# Box of Shame:

## A Memoir of Addiction, Survival, and Forgiveness

Anita Ball

Box of Shame


Independently published in Canada. Requests may be submitted by email to: anitakball@yahoo.com

First edition, 2021

ISBN: (Paperback Book)
978-17776374-3-9

ISBN: (Hardcover Book)
978-1-7776374-2-2

*"I would rather go through life sober, believing I'm an alcoholic, than go through life drunk, trying to convince myself that I'm not."*

*Anonymous*

# CONTENTS

# INTRODUCTION

Digging up the past can be a painful journey. At some point, the past should remain behind us as a distant memory. However, facing our demons head-on, can begin the path of healing. Secrecy does not beget healing, so this story is told with brutal honesty and respect from my memory and experiences; there is no other way. The stories within this text are true, although names and some details have been altered to protect the identity of certain individuals.

My hope is to bring forth a better understanding of addiction and mental illness to others. I hid behind the walls of stigma that still exist today. Stigma prevents people from reaching out and achieving real freedom. It is not my intention to paint a picture-perfect ending. Even though I have made it through to sobriety, this does not mean that my struggles are over. Focusing on self-care is a lifelong process. Depression still strikes and life can get overwhelming, but I am alive, I have a roof over my head and love all around me. If my story touches one life, then my struggles were worth it.

These words may not make for an easy read for some. Addiction is a dark world filled with shame and a code of silence. Buried secrets, especially the most painful ones, are a soul killer, so fully releasing the past, is part of my ongoing self-care and freedom.

Through the ugliness of alcoholism, life provided me with hidden blessings along the way to remind me that hope is always alive. A faint sparkle of light came at just the right moments. At the time of writing this book, I've been sober for 25 years; the strength of my foundation has stood the test of time. I would never travel back in time to change my past, out of fear that this exact instance would not exist because, at this moment, I am sober and free.

Chapter 1

# POISON

In a whisper, the words, "I think I'm going to die," came out as I clutched my knees to my chest, trying to rock the pain away. Poison was racing through my veins, but no one dies from alcohol; at least that's what I believed. By 8 o'clock, I had lost myself. I went from tipsy silliness at the dinner table to groaning in agony. Fear started to invade my body, as this was not the silliness I had expected. My boyfriend Tony escorted me to the antique Victorian couch, and Mrs. Brunetti put a cool cloth on my forehead. A phone call was made, from one European parent with broken English to another. The message was understood; "Anita sick, come now." *Click.*

My elderly father was the one who came to the rescue, as he was the licensed driver of our household and the authoritarian, much like his own father. He came to Christ in his twenties and was of the Finnish Free Church denomination. Disciples of the congregation would spread the good news about the savior Jesus Christ and Dad was a disciple. Being drunk by the spirit was allowed, but not by alcohol. It was the seed to destruction in his mind.

We lived in a city called Thunder Bay, in Ontario, with a population of about 110,000. The city rested on the northern shores of Lake Superior, where the waterfront's breeze would feel refreshing during a humid day. We experienced all four seasons; spring, summer, fall, and winter. This is an appealing attraction for hunters and fishermen from near and far, including our friendly neighbors from America. We were home to one of Canadas greatest natural wonders, the Sleeping Giant, which is a rock peninsula in the shape of a giant laying on its back. The legend of how the giant came to be is a fascinating story told by the Ojibway elders as early as the late 1800s. The area has been a popular campground for years, with miles of scenic hiking trails. There was much to enjoy in our town, known as the city with a giant heart. My dad should have been enjoying these glories since retiring, but instead he was trying to save me. My father arrived at the off-white brick residence on Melbourne Drive. A few blossoming apple trees on the front lawn were almost ready to be harvested. Decorative cascading vines dangled along the high cedar fence. Vegetation was still blooming near the end of the summer, and a large pot of vivid petunias gave a delightfully fragrant touch right at the entrance doormat that read, "WELCOME."

Dad parked on the street with one tire perched on the curb; he marched to the side door, let himself in without knocking, stopped on the small landing, anxious. He had no idea what to expect or what sickness I had. My dad hesitated to step up into the kitchen or walk down the stairwell to the basement. He paused there and yelled, "Anita!" Tony's dad hollered from the den, "Anita's here." My boyfriend appeared at the bottom of the staircase, flagging him down. Dad followed him to my side, and at first glance, he knew what caused my illness. He wanted me out of the house of evil as fast as possible. My cheeks glowed as if I'd applied too much blush, my eyes were droopy and filled with red spider veins. In my semi-conscious state, my boyfriend tried to shake me back into reality while his teeth tried to control his twitching lower lip.

"Anita, come on, snap out of it… sorry, but I didn't know what else to do; we had to call your parents."

I could only let out a groan. *They called my dad? Anyone but him!* Dad was hot-tempered, and unpredictable. He did not want his children to drink; it was evil. The Brunetti family didn't want the responsibility of nursing me back to health. They had no choice but to give me up to my father.

Mr. Brunetti's hands waved about in front of him, as he tried to explain what happened. He spoke with passion, regardless of the topic. He was a proud Italian man. Mr. B went on about dinner and my lack of tolerance to the homemade wine. I'm sure my dad didn't understand all of the conversation, but it was clear when Tony's Dad said, "she drink too much wine." Both men were aging fathers. They tried to enforce strict rules with their children, but there was one big difference between the two Dads: alcohol. Mine saw it as poison and as a sin; Tony's dad spent months at a time producing it for his family. Sometimes Tony would sneak a small bottle of wine to school, "red or white?" he'd ask me. *Oh, how I loved that boy*. The cellar held several glorious five-gallon glass carboys: red wine, white wine, and moonshine. One whiff of moonshine almost knocked me off my feet; I'd have to work my way up to that.

The two men stood in front of the couch talking, while Tony's mom put another fresh cool cloth, on my forehead. Their bodies appeared to swivel about, and I couldn't tell one dad from the other. My dad tried to ask why I was drinking in their home. Both men spoke broken English. Mr. B's first language was Italian, and my dad spoke Finnish. I couldn't make out most of the conversation, and the room was zooming around me. The last thing I heard came from my dad, "Seee no more rrrink!"

Tony helped me to my feet and Dad took over. I used every ounce of energy to stand and not land on the floor. I'd never be able to walk a straight line, but I willed one foot in front of the other. With Dad's help, I got partway up the stairs until my legs collapsed beneath me. He caught my lethargic body and carried me to the truck. I was just under five feet tall and hardly 100lbs, but with a belly full of wine, I must've doubled my weight. Dad was about 5 feet 4 inches, but he seemed much bigger. I'd seen him stack heavy log after log, with a hook, all day long as if they were pencils. Big heavy chainsaws, sledgehammers, skidder chains; what he lacked in stature, he made up for in pure determination - and he was determined to get me out of there.

I did not talk, because my mouth would not articulate any sensible words. I did what I could to behave like a sober human being. I thought I was tricking him, but it was quite obvious that I did not have a stomach bug. Seatbelts were optional, but he buckled me in to keep me in place. On the drive home, I faintly heard his matter-of-fact words, "you will never go there again." He was upset and disappointed. Grade nine was about to begin, and my parents had discovered my secret drinking. I stared out the window, hoping the drive home would be in silence, as I watched the neighborhood houses pass by in a blurry haze. We arrived at a stop sign by a mini mall, with a billboard advertising free wine tasting. My stomach curdled at the thought. My belly was a storming ocean, and I was getting seasick.

Dad knew how to drive a skidder through bushy terrain, but he was terrible at city driving. He had his own rule book for driving; red means go, and green means stop. Sometimes I thought he was color blind. Both feet battled the gas and the brake. He must have got his driver's license from a cereal box! My stomach couldn't handle his usual erratic driving today; queasiness stirred. Acidic juices hit my throat, and out came the spaghetti and red liquid splashing onto my lap and the door. The rancid smell caused another explosion of vomit. I wanted to die. I was poisoned. This was the dawn of my drinking career at 14 years old.

When I was a child, my parents forbid alcohol in our household. I didn't understand what evil it possessed. As a Christian family, we accepted that Jesus changed water into wine, so wine should be a part of our way of life. In moderation, where is the harm? Moderation was not a word in my vocabulary. Sadly, social drinking would never be a part of my story. The moment I had a taste of sweet champagne and the pleasant whirlwind ride it offered me, I needed more. Alcohol made me brave and helped to hide my painful past that no one knew about. It became my best friend; it turned tears into laughter, tucked away unpleasant memories, and boosted my confidence. The hangovers and other hassles that came along with it were trivial in comparison.

The rest of the evening turned into a drunken blur. Dad made sure I made it downstairs to my bed, in one piece. I passed out until about two in the morning. I awoke and staggered to the shower to wash the sticky vomit out of my hair. The next day, I woke up at noon with a pounding headache and full of regret about my dad seeing me drunk. I needed coffee. I wrapped my soft blue housecoat around me and walked up the stairs, using the handrail to avoid falling. I did not want to face my parents, especially my dad.

My mom handed me a mug, while barely looking at me. "Have some coffee." She continued with the dishes, deep in concentration. I felt a heaviness of shame coming from her, or was it a blanket of relief that I was safe and sound under her roof? Either way, I was in no mood to engage in conversation with my pounding headache and sprouting hormones. Mom kept to herself and let Dad do the talking. I wondered what my dad had told her. I poured steaming hot coffee into my mug and flavored it with three heaping spoons of sugar. Finns love their coffee as much as their saunas; the stronger, the better. As a young girl, Mom would pour me half a cup, and I'd drop in two cubes of sugar and enjoy it with pulla; a sweet coffee bread commonly found in Finnish homes - some traditions never die.

Dad sat at the table with his plastic reading glasses about to slip off from the tip of his nose. He was reading the Finnish newspaper. Without looking up, he said, "Alcohol is poison, did you know that?" Here we go; the lecture was coming. I replied, "Yeah, sure, poison is being sold in the stores, and people are drinking it! We are being murdered!" The old man conjured up some crazy ideas, and this theory was one of them. I rolled my eyes and waited for him to respond. "One day, when you have some brains in your head, you'll learn. Brats like you don't know nothing," he said in a huff as he pushed up his glasses, lowered his paper, and added, "you will not go back to that boy's house." That boy's house was the gateway to my drinking, according to him. Both my hands wrapped around the warm mug, my slouched back perked up, "Oh, yes, I will! You can't stop me!" Did he think his words would keep me from my boyfriend? He'd taken this too far. I was a teen girl madly in love. He dropped his paper, stood up, and went to the kitchen window. "Do you see those telephone lines out there?" I briefly looked in his direction but did not respond. Whatever the meaning of the telephone lines was, it was not going to be remotely normal. "If I catch you at his house, I will hang his balls over those wires!" He gave me a smirk of satisfaction.

I looked at mom and yelled, "Mom, Isä's crazy!" Isä translates to father in Finnish, and this is how my siblings and I always addressed him. I went to pout in the living room. Mom stopped her humming at the kitchen sink and said, “Yes, I know, but we didn’t even know where you were yesterday, until Mr. Brunetti called us.” She knew Dad well; she knew his temper and that sometimes he would come through on his threats. Her attempts at talking sense into him had failed many times over the past thirty years, so she would pick her battles. She was much more level-headed than he was.

I could still hear him rambling on about what boys want to do to young girls. This was a conversation I was not going to have with my dad, but I was thinking, *Isä, I want him to do those things to me!* I knew I would do everything in my power to keep us together. He was my first love, but I now had a new fear. Yesterday, the Brunettis gave Dad their address to pick me up, so he could now show up at any time. Next time, he would not be pleasant. I avoided Tony’s place for a while, in fear of my dad’s threat. We spent our time together at school or the park. Dad would never sign me out of school just to separate us, because he saw what an education can do. His first born graduated with a teaching degree and the second one with a nursing degree. I was supposed to follow in those footsteps. He probably felt some assurance that the adult supervision at school would deter bad behaviors like drinking.

One terrible drunken experience didn't push me away from drinking. Most of my peers were doing it, so it did not feel that unusual. Some of my siblings had experienced it and turned out to be social drinkers as adults. I never imagined that I would be much different. The drinking scene was a passage that teens would go through. Some escaped it, but I was on a mission. I had a one-way ticket to party town. For me, it didn't take long to realize that alcohol was soothing my emptiness, calming my anxiety, and I couldn't foresee ever giving it up; I was hooked rather quickly. I spent my days planning how and where alcohol would be available to me; I worshiped it. While my peers also drank, most seemed to have a little more balance. They had part-time jobs or did sports. Their lives included alcohol-free activities. Me, not as much. When I wasn't drinking, I was thinking about it.

I never dreamt that drinking would harm me more than a nasty hangover. I could not predict damaging effects, such as breaking my parent's hearts, lying, stealing, and throwing away every moral and value I'd been taught. I didn't know I'd be a slave to the bottle to face myself daily. No, these are not the dreams of a little girl, but addiction cleverly snuck in and gave false promises of confidence and beauty. My dreams were of the white picket fence variety, my one and only true love, and a house full of children. Despite a rough start to life,

I still believed I would have the all-Canadian normal life; that somehow, I would pass through the teenage portal and be normal, like everyone else before me. I'd be successful. Happy. That's how it ends. I was a good Sunday school girl, said my prayers with my mom, and was content.

Country living, outdoor play, and a good dose of vitamin D was my life. Childhood seemed amazing at a glance but, venturing deeper things were not as they appeared.

Chapter 2

# CITY BORN; COUNTRY RAISED

In April of 1973, my mom was admitted to the hospital. She was secretly in the last trimester of pregnancy, with no obvious signs of expecting. My sisters speculated about our mother's widened girth and sudden disappearance from the home, but it was not clear what her condition was. She was experiencing preeclampsia, which is a serious pregnancy complication that can be dangerous to both mother and child; it can even result in death. Preeclampsia is marked by hypertension. The only cure is to give birth as soon as possible. She was monitored for a few weeks and then scheduled for a cesarian section, to safely deliver me. Mom and I were brought home on a lovely spring day, to my brother's complete shock. He had no inclination of my mom being pregnant and believed that she was sick and needed to rest at the hospital. No one expected another sister at moms age of 44. My mom didn't share much information; she'd rather surprise everyone.

The clan consisted of seven children at home, and I now made eight, two siblings had passed before me. My dad was thrilled to have another beautiful baby, telling everyone he'd been given the best 50th birthday present ever. Our house was modest, and as the tribe grew, new walls divided the boys from the girls. Finnish was the primary language spoken, and we learned English in school. Both parents immigrated from Finland to Canada in 1960, with six offspring in tow. Friends of my parents sent word to them about the booming forestry industry in Canada, and they knew they had to make the move to create a better life. The large family arrived in the prairies of Saskatoon, Saskatchewan, moving around a few times before I was born.

My parents had pennies, when they arrived in a foreign country, but with a will and a strong faith, they thrived. Without relatives or friends nearby, the transition was tough for a young family. They connected with earlier Finnish immigrants, whom they could communicate with and receive support from the culture shock of moving to another country. Eventually, Dad found work at Great Lakes Paper Mill and in bush camps, which provided for the growing household. The camps were located in out-lying forestry areas where there was a high demand for bush-workers. With his chainsaw, Dad would cut trees, strip them by hand, and have them ready for pick-up by logging trucks.

My mom raised us by herself, for the most part. A house full of screaming kids, and no support from her other half, must have been stressful. The fight to be heard became the battle amongst a slew of kids. The household volume would escalate, and Dad's yelling for silence didn't help. Brothers stood against sisters; high heels and knives fired through the air like missiles, and a substantial amount of door slamming echoed throughout the tiny house. This was the unpredictable zoo I was thrown into; everyone fought to be heard and valued. Our overcrowded existence created hard times and limited funds, but in the words of Robert H. Schuller, "Tough times never last, but tough people do!" This was us.

In the summer of 1976, we moved to the boonies, a small community just beyond the city, called Kaministiquia (Cam-i-nist-i-qwa). It could be a tongue twister for a youngster, but by the time I started school, I knew how to pronounce it and spell it correctly. The population was not more than 200 people at the time. A community hall was nearby for local events, like dances and dinners. The closest variety store was five miles away, down the highway. Kam, which is what everyone called it, was barely a dot on the map.

The older siblings had already left the nest and would not experience country living. *What a shame*. They were stuck with next-door neighbors, noisy city streets, and nothing to do. I had animals, miles of freedom, rivers to explore, and forts to build, all just outside my door. They had a different outlook – the city life perspective. The eldest was married, others had established their lives and jobs, and one teenage sister became a mom. Our home had now downsized to three children still in the nest. Jari was ten, sister Niina, fifteen, and I, the baby of the family, was three.

With a bush worker's wage, and Mom no longer working due to the move, purchasing a home would not be an option. So how does a family obtain a house without funding? A wee birdy delivered a message to my dad's ear about an elderly couple living in the country who wished to retire to the city. My dad said it was a message from God himself. Dad met with the Viitalaa's, details were discussed, and with a handshake, the old farmhouse on Hill Road belonged to us. It came complete with a massive barn of bulls, chickens, a Shetland pony and a goat. It was a house-for-a house switch, so money was not exchanged. The elderly couple would take our small house in Thunder Bay, and we would live in the farmhouse. The house swap made sense, because the Viitalaa's needed city life in their senior years, and my parents craved the country.

The house lacked livability in many ways; sawdust and newspapers filled the walls, acting as insulation. There was an old oil furnace that would keep the home heated, when it worked. An indoor wood stove was common for country houses, but this place did not have one. There were some perks though, like nooks and crannies for extra storage in the most unusual places. A sliding two-foot door in the wall of the small hallway near my parent's bedroom was like a secret hideout. The house had a basement, main floor, and an upper level with two bedrooms. There was no bathroom, bathing was done in the sauna and when nature called, we would use the outhouse.

Through blistery snow or torrential rains, we had to walk a few hundred feet to the barn where the bulls and chickens lived. The outhouse was next to the barn, which was fenced for the bulls. At one bathroom visit, Mom and I spent a few minutes checking on the animals, before heading back to the house. There were light grey clouds in the sky when we entered the barn, but when we were about to leave, the clouds grew black and angry, and a downpour began. Mom opened the red barn door, and the wind almost ripped the door off the building. She struggled for a moment to shut the door against the strong wind and rain that pelted her in the face. I looked up at her in admiration, *my mom may be little, but she is so strong and brave.*

"We can't go out there; we will have to wait until it slows down." Mom's words were calm, and I knew I was safe. I peeked through the cracks of the barn boards and could see darkness. Trees swayed back and forth, looking like they may snap at any second. The rain was fierce for several minutes, and every time I asked Mom if we could go back to the house, she said we couldn't. Finally, the pounding rain eased up a touch, and we made a run for it. She opened the door and yelled, "Let's go! We have to run fast like we're in a race!" I ran with my hands waving in the air to feel the raindrops, and stomping into every puddle I could find, as we passed the abandoned milk house and garage. Mom was trying to cover her head with her purple T-shirt. We laughed as we got soaked from head to toe, while running towards the house. Every time I went to the outhouse, I picture us laughing and racing down the foot path in the rain. This would not be our last time running together for safety.

There wasn't much to the rest of the house. The kitchen had a small old fridge and a stove, but not the electric kind. There was an antique wood-burning oven, a fire hazard for a small kitchen. Meal preparation took planning and time. My mom would move the heavy top and light a fire in the box. When the wood became hot coals, she could boil water or bake bread in the oven. This would also help to take the chill out of the air on frigid days. In the winter, the pipes often froze, so we would have no running water, but snow could always be melted in a large pot on the stove.

My favorite area was on the landing of the L-shaped staircase that went to the upper level. By mid-afternoon the beaming sun shone through the picture window, and I'd practice coloring in the lines, as I was told to do. In an undetectable motion, the bubbly clouds would float above the tall barn straight ahead. The garage doors, positioned to the left by the road, were usually open, exposing the green and yellow John Deere tractor. The view was simple; grass, trees, gravel, and a few outdoor structures. Peaceful.

Out of us three kids, I took to the country lifestyle the quickest. I'd only spent the first few years in tight quarters, so the change of scenery came easily to me, but not so much for my sister and brother. Jari did not have a bedroom at first, so he had to sleep on the floor on a mattress between

Niina's room and my parents' room. My bed was at the foot end of my parents' bed, separated by a curtain tacked to the ceiling. It was a metal bed frame, with a springy metal hammock, instead of a mattress and a few extra blankets and rugs to cushion my body. Niina had her own room with a door for privacy that had a fancy glass doorknob and a proper bed, but she hated the farmhouse. Solitude, a run-down house and stinky farm animals were not her style. Niina's friends lived in the city. Casual phone calls to Thunder Bay could not be made, because they cost money, and my parents had to pinch every cent; only emergency calls were allowed. She was disconnected from the world.

Surrounded by bush, limited amenities, and cold winter nights was how we rolled. Mice lived in the walls and scurried through the kitchen cupboards. Within a year, Niina packed a bag, walked to the highway, thumbed a ride into town, and shacked up with her boyfriend, who later became her husband. Jari was happy because he now had the only private bedroom. Niina remained a regular presence in my childhood, visiting often and taking me on city adventures wearing corduroy pants, a fancy purse, and usually high heels. Such a fashionable chick, and kind of like a mother figure to me, along with my other sisters.

My sisters and brothers helped to take care of me. My life was sheltered, and communication between my parents and the world was limited. The generation gap between myself and my parents was wide, but my siblings were up-to-date with kids in the 70s and 80s. They gave me opportunities they did not have, like teaching me how to roller skate, swim, and downhill ski. Our parents could never have afforded these luxuries. Roller skates, swim lessons, and ski equipment for all the kids were not even a consideration; food and shelter were the priority. My siblings had to seek out free entertainment or get a job to pay for their own activities, and they did. I was the baby of the family, whom they spoiled. I had more food, more toys, and sometimes even new clothes; this was impossible when there were many mouths to feed.

Life in Kam was pretty great. I was surrounded by God's green earth; I had a stay-at-home mom while Dad worked, and with miles between neighbors, we could do whatever we wanted. Fears of traffic or police were hardly ever a thought. Although, sometimes nosey neighbors or a casual drive-by from law enforcement wouldn't have been a bad idea; maybe then Dad's punishments would have softened somewhat.

## Box of Shame

Dad's hot temper could ignite at the most innocent things; things that a child could never understand. He had once spotted pink nail polish on my fingers, and he screamed, "only whores wear nail polish!" He grabbed my hand and spat on my fingers, trying to take the polish off. I didn't know what a "whore" was, but by Dad's reaction, it had to be something bad; therefore, I was bad. That was the overwhelming message of my childhood, but sometimes he had reason to explode, like when his hard work completely crumbled to the ground, literally.

Chapter 3

# THE GREENHOUSE

The country lifestyle, was the only way my parents wanted to live, as their childhoods were rooted in the farm lands of Finland. They never did enjoy city living in Canada, but in the early years, it was the most convenient lifestyle. Thunder Bay had a large community of Finnish immigrants, and Mom was able to work in restaurants to help provide for the growing family. When Dad was in the bush, she could walk to work, and the older siblings were head of the household while she was gone.

In Kam, Dad would be the sole provider, so Mom could get back into gardening. With the limitations of living on small city lots, her previous gardens could only produce so many potatoes, but now she had room for a large crop. She had the acreage and more time. Mom oversaw the animals and worked alongside my dad, mending fences, building sheds, shoveling snow, and so much more. Hard work fuelled her spirit, but she and Dad argued when they teamed up on projects. He would scream, curse, and throw things. When she couldn't handle him anymore, she would sarcastically laugh, and Dad would get even more steamed.

## Box of Shame

Dad had started a small renovation project by the stairs. The old walls needed new paneling. His assistant was not helping in the way he wanted, so he began screaming at her. He reached for his knife and scratched the wall in a mad frenzy, leaving deep grooves in the paneling. He stabbed the knife into the wall, leaving it vibrating back and forth while he stormed off yelling, "you fix it then!" I inspected the damage, and a new panel would be needed, in which he later replaced. I couldn't understand why he would destroy his own work, creating more work for himself in the long run. Mom said he was *hullu.* (crazy)

Building a greenhouse for my mom was another project my dad had planned. Mom had a green thumb or two, and we always had fresh vegetables; potatoes, carrots, peas, onions, and beets often ended up on the dinner table. Having a greenhouse would make growing vegetables much easier. Over the next two years, Dad collected windowpanes from anywhere he could find them. He gathered odd sizes and scraps of lumber for the job, and he worked on the structure until snow covered the hills. It was finally ready for the spring.

I had a glass house to play in, and Mom started her seedlings for the summer. The structure was nothing to brag about. Dad wasn't much of a carpenter, but for me, as I stood inside the glass walls, I was protected from the wind and the rain; fragile and magnificent, this was something I'd never seen until then. I was about six, when I was playing in the glass house, and I noticed some cracks in the corner. I tapped at it with my finger until it shattered. The lovely tinkle and shimmering shards of glass, looked like a box of jewels. I tried to poke what was left in the windowpane with my hands but decided I needed a tool. The garage had what I needed. I grabbed an ax to clean out the remaining sharp edges. The busting of glass continued onward. I don't know why I attacked the house, as I didn't feel angry. Perhaps, I just wanted to listen to the musical dance of shattering glass. I swung at the next windowpane with the ax in hand, and it resembled the notes of a symphony, pleasing to my ears. The urge to smash the remaining windows was impossible to ignore. One by one, the smashing continued until only a mountain of bling remained. The entire structure had fallen by my hands. It wasn't long before Dad came rolling into the driveway and saw the pile of rubble.

He jumped out of the truck, slammed the door, and the screaming began; and it wasn't just him. I ran for my life. The crack of a whip cut the air behind me as Dad chased me throughout the house and up the stairs, with a black rubber oil hose.

A fluttering wind floated by my arm, followed by a fierce echoing, *SNAP*. By the time he got to the top stair, his breath had become heavy, and he rested. I made it to the bedroom and slid under the bed into home base. *Safe*. In silence, I cried and wished that my mom would stop him or some force of nature would split the house in two with him on the other side. I knew I should not have trashed the greenhouse, but I just hoped he would not kill me. Would he whip me or strangle me? I felt trapped. My only plan was to glue myself to the metal foot of the bed and hope that it would somehow shield me. I laid on my stomach with my elbows tight against my sides, ankles crossed. My hands were tightly clasped together in prayer, with the dust bunnies telling my body to stop shaking. After he caught his breath, around the bend, he came. His footsteps entered the room, slowly coming towards the bed, and then they stopped. I squeezed my eyes tight, and anticipated he would make this into a dramatic game of hide and seek.

"Anita, come out from your hiding spot." His stern voice meant business. *I can't show myself, I just can't*. His demeanor was mellow, and this wasn't good. I'd lay like a statue for the rest of my life if I had to; I couldn't trust him. Tears splattered onto the wood floor, as seconds seemed like hours. I didn't answer. I just waited for his next move. Then oddly, he turned around and left. I don't know what made him change direction, but I had a silent sigh of relief. I cannot say what he would have done with the hose, but his voice and intimidation tactics were frightening enough.

I stayed in hiding, until a slight vibration from the slamming exterior door hit my body. He would be outside for a while. Today I escaped him. I scurried to Jari's empty room, shut the door, and sat on his bed. His room was small - the size of a closet, but I liked it, mainly because he had one. I looked through a few Hardy Boys books on Jari's bookshelf and thought about telling him about the hose when he got home. But, why? If Mom couldn't stop Dad from raging, our voices would not make one bit of difference. We were powerless kids, too scared to speak until we grew and found the courage to protest when Dad had gone too far.

Chapter 4

# JINGLE BELLS

Fall had come. I was around eight years old, when something about our typical family began to feel not so typical. Jari and I wanted to be like all kids, to fit in. Physical discipline at home or school was common in our days, and it was hardly ever discussed; all emotions were stuffed inside. Our culture and personalities expected that feelings would be hidden away in darkness. Jari was tight-lipped when it came to talking about emotional matters, especially when it came to Dad, until one day he let our dad have it.

My class began preparing for our annual Christmas concert. Christmas was exciting, but I was not too thrilled about standing in front of a crowd of parents, singing and dancing for them. Our concert would be held at our community center. Each class rehearsed for months and would have a chance to perform at the beginning of December. In October, we started preparing our costumes. The girls all had red Santa hats and red skirts. We had vests with Christmas decorations randomly pinned in the front and thick white leggings. For a little extra pizzaz, our teacher gave us bells attached to elastic bands that we would wear on our wrists and ankles. Before we would even be seen on the stage, we would be heard. As terrifying as it was to have all eyes on me, I was happy with our song choices and dance choreography. School productions were a big event, particularly in Kam, as it was a tight nit community. People gathered for all sorts of occasions, just to mingle with their neighbors. We were allowed to bring our costumes home so that we could practice the routine on our own time. I walked around jingling my bells, even when I was not practicing. Around this time, we had a female calico who had six fluffy kittens. Dad was not a cat lover, more of a cat hater, but he tolerated them for a while. When the kittens were old enough, at about four or five weeks, they could be trained to wear collars. Whoever would adopt the kittens, would appreciate it. Of course, I hoped that we would keep at least one of them, but that would not be possible. I would love them until it was adoption time.

I didn't have any collars, but I did have four elastic bands with bells on them. This was the perfect solution; they could wear the elastic bands, and I'd be able to hear them from afar. They looked so adorable, with the bells dangling in front of their fuzzy chests. The kittens were getting rambunctious, running around the room, making a mess in the littler box, and meowing. They were not allowed anywhere except the spare room where they were born. When Mom heard their whining, she told me, “The kittens must be quiet, or else Isä will get angry.” She feared his anger and what he might do with the kittens.

The evening was dark, and it was around 9 o’clock when I saw my dad marching down the hallway holding three kittens in his hands. His face was devoid of expression. He was in a trance-like state. He was on a mission. I panicked and raced to his side, screaming, “What are you doing!” He ignored me. I latched onto the crook of his arm, “Nooo, nooo, let them go!” My feet left the floor as I tried to straighten his arm to free the kittens, but he had arms of steel. I wailed in distress and called for Jari’s help but it was too late. Dad shook his bionic arm, until he was free of the hanging nuisance and opened the door. The wind whisked the hammering rain drops from the truck to the shed as he wound up and threw each kitten out into the night, into the abyss. Dad went back for the remaining kittens. As he passed by his two hysterical children, with terrified kittens in his hands, Jari snarled at him, “I’m going to call the police, and you’re going to jail!”

“Go ahead, call. The police are not coming!” Dad whips the last of the kitties out the door. My tears turn into anger, but I was thrilled that Jari was threatening him.

"Jari, do it, call them! He's crazy. He's a murderer!" I step closer to Jari and shove him towards the kitchen where the phone is.

Jari wipes his face with his sleeve. With his eyes still welled up, he says, "This is animal cruelty. Do you know that this is against the law?!" Jari was fifteen years old, so he knew what he was talking about.

"You tell him! Tell him he's going to be in jail forever!" Jari looks me in my swollen eyes. I was proud to call him my brother.

"How will you survive if I go to jail?" Dad asked. We lived in the sticks, our mom didn't drive, and she only spoke Finnish. How would we get food, wood, or a paycheck? Our lives would be ruined - that fact stopped us from making the call. Dad and his righteous ego won again.

He went to his room and slammed the door. I hollered to Jari and my mom in the kitchen, saying, "I'm going to find the kittens."

"No, you're not." My mom said. "Let them go. It is dark and stormy out there, and you won't be able to find them. They are dead." She wanted to put this terrible night behind us.

Nothing could be done at this point to erase the nightmare we all just witnessed. I hoped that they may have survived. I waited a little while and then snuck out with a flashlight, walking past the driveway, over the lawn and down the embankment where they had been thrown. The pounding of the rain would have drowned out any final cries if there were any. The long grass and spots of slippery clay made it impossible to search for long. Not a trace existed. The heavy downpour killed my light. I was in the dark, other than the odd flash of lightning, mourning the lost kittens, utterly distraught. Then I remembered, my jingle bells for the Christmas concert were on the kittens.

Chapter 5

## THE CHAINSAW MASTER

The time had come. "Does everyone have their costumes?" asked Mrs. Sifton in her cheery, festive voice. I looked down at my desk, trying to avoid eye contact. Everyone else in the class would have their bells except for me. I hoped my teacher would not make a big deal out of this. I couldn't tell her where my bells were. A little white lie would be okay, by just saying that I lost them. Without question, she replaced my bells. *Thank you, Mrs. Sifton.* The traumatizing kitten episode went straight into my already formed box of shame. How can a father do such hurtful things? Did he love me at all? These were questions that were never answered when I was a child. However, I did see that he was capable of love. He had five grandchildren who adored him. They softened his heart, and they never experienced his lunacies. Sure, they saw his fits of anger and bullheadedness, but they didn't know the whole story. They were lucky to have a hardworking, jolly old man, with a side of crazy, to call Pappa.

His first grandchild was unexpected. It was a tough time for my sister, being a teen mom, and she felt obligated to marry her boyfriend due to pressure from my parents. But when Ritchie was born, Mom and Dad were thrilled. My mom was pregnant with me, and I was born two months later, becoming Auntie Anita the second I entered the world. My nephew spent a lot of time with us at the farmhouse, and we had some memorable moments. I loved hanging out with him and playing trucks or army dudes. We would play in the mud and did whatever we wanted in the barn or the garage.

Dad had interesting tools and gadgets in the garage. There were shelves lined with paints and solvents of every kind: —oils, cleaners, sprays, everything that a garage needed. Ritchie and I created imaginary games of cops and robbers or war. I can't quite remember the reasoning of our four-year-old minds, but we needed "things" from the garage. An arsenal of protection from the *robbers* possibly, surely Dad would not mind us borrowing what we needed. Ritchie was the taller one of us, so he could reach for the shiny can on the work bench. We opened the can, and it spilled onto his leg. The rocks in his pocket got wet, so he took them out, and we continued. We did not realize what damage was occurring onto his thigh beneath his pants. Sometimes, injuries can occur without pain.

Later that evening, Ritchie's mom picked him up, and they went home. During the usual bedtime routine of bathing and PJ's, my sister noticed a reddened area on his thigh and an odd scent on his almost dry jeans. Ritchie could not explain the inflammation, so off to the hospital they went. After a thorough investigation by my parents in the garage, it was determined that the scent came from Erusticator Rust Removal. It has a high concentration of hydrofluoric acid, powerful enough to etch glass, but Ritchie was too involved with our play time to notice any burning. His thigh suffered chemical burns, and the scars remained into adulthood.

After the accident, my sister told our mom to keep an eye on us kids. Mom tried, but we were sneaky, and her parenting style was pretty slack. It wouldn't take long until Ritchie, and I would find trouble, yet again. My dad always had oil pails scattered around the garage for his equipment. Ritchie and I decided it would be a good idea to squeeze ourselves into an empty five-gallon metal oil pail. He hesitated, but I showed him how to do it. "Go like this Ritchie," I steadied the pail with my hands, "step in with one foot, then put the other foot in and sit down, easy as pie." We would pretend we were monkeys in a barrel and roll down the driveway. Oh, what fun this would be! I got out and let him have his turn. He climbed in, and I smiled and cheered until he tried to get out. "I can't get out," he said.

I laughed and rolled my eyes. "Sure, you can't. You're just bugging, right? Ritchie ignored me, as he tried to push up, while he grunted. He wasn't laughing.

"I think I'm really stuck," he said, as he tried to wiggle his little body free. I held his hands and tried to pull him, then pushed the pail onto its side, but nothing would work. "You have to try harder, Ritchie," I pleaded.

Grown-up involvement was the last resort, because I didn't want to be in trouble. After several attempts and Ritchie's growing anxiety, we needed adult help. With great hesitation, I found an adult – my dad. I ran to Ritchie to tell him my dad was coming. He was relieved that help was on the way, but I feared what his reaction would be when he saw Ritchie stuck in a pail. At the very least, he would scream at us rotten kids. Of course, it would be my fault. Dad came out and assessed the situation and muttered away about us "damn brats", while trying to get Ritchie out without ripping his arms off, but he made no headway. As he walked away, he shouted in his best English words, “no take pails!”

Ritchie was on the verge of tears now, but I see that he was trying hard to be brave. Minutes later, Dad returned with a chainsaw! It was worse than I feared; now we’re dead! My eyes widened in terror. For a split second, I thought he might cut him in half. Why else would he get a chainsaw? I stood close to my mom as my little heart thumped faster. *Calm down; it’s ok, he’s not going to cut him in half; he’s not that crazy!* With all the commotion and hearing his Pappa’s angry words, Ritchie fainted at the sound of the chainsaws rumble, and his head flopped to the side. His mom cradled his limp body. I yanked my mom’s arm and screamed, “Look! Look! Is he ok?” My mom quickly reassures me that he just went into a deep sleep and would be fine. I didn’t know how this might work without blood spill, but my dad, the chainsaw master, knew exactly what to do.

My sister wrapped a blanket around Ritchie’s limp upper body. Pappa delicately touched the speeding chain to the metal, and sparks hit the sky. I covered my eyes with my palms, too scared to look. The high-pitched screeching of the chainsaw stung my ears. The cutting continued to the bottom of the pail, then Dad worked with his hands, rolling away the sharp edges. Ritchie was safe. His Pappa skillfully carved him out of a pail, like a master woodsman carving a totem poll. Not a hair on his body was harmed. Ritchie was brought to the couch to recover. Thankfully, Dad was home, acted quickly and knew how to save Ritchie. He sat in the recliner near Ritchie and lets out a jovial laugh of relief. I was glad to hear his chuckle because he could've lost his temper about this. I could never estimate what circumstance he would be okay with and what would cause his raging. "Jumping into pails isn't so fun now, is it?" He snickered.

I sat on the floor, waiting for Ritchie's eyes to open. "No, we will never do that again." I wondered if any other dads would know what to do when a boy is stuck in a pail? That day Isä was my hero. Sadly, it would be years before I ever had those thoughts again.

Chapter 6

# JARI

Isä, my father, was born on December 13, 1923, in rural Finland into a family of eight children. He was the eldest. Times were challenging, especially for families with little money and low status. Food was not abundant, and the family held nothing of value to their name. They survived on a traveling preacher's wage. My grandfather preached the word of the bible in the homes of those who welcomed him. This work hardly provided life's necessities like food. World War Two was approaching and my dad lied about his age to join the army at the tender age of sixteen. He would fight for his country and his family to have freedoms they never had before, and he would get fed. Had he known he would be thrown into the front lines and experience horrific brutalities that would forever haunt him, he may have made a different choice.

When young men left to serve their countries, many did not return home. Some of my dad's friends lost their lives in the fight. Dad survived, almost without wounds. His body escaped, but not his mind. The brutality of war damaged the psyche of men. Liquor and drugs would help to numb the images etched into their brains. Unfortunately, limited resources, lack of knowledge, and stigma stood in the way of any meaningful recovery or healing.

Sometime after the war, God reached out to Dad, and he accepted the help of God. He described it as a divine moment that literally knocked him off his bike as he pedaled to a local bar – one of the roughest in the area. The audible voice of God spoke to him, asking, "where are you going?" He got back onto his bike, changed his route, and went home. Did he escape a fatal night? God works in mysterious ways. Although life would still be challenging, Dad was a changed man. He believed in healing and forgiveness. He often spoke of his divine intervention in church and was interviewed on a local Christian TV station. He spent a lifetime, with a strong conviction that he would always have healing, and it was proven to him many times over with physical pains but, his mental health issues remained. Didn't he realize he needed healing of a deeper sort? Discussing feelings of turmoil was never a topic. He was a man's man and was expected to hide emotions, but pain and anger cannot live within for long. Feelings erupted, often directed at his children in coldness and heartless behaviors. I witnessed Dad's explosions more than I'd like to admit.

After Niina left, Jari and I were the only ones left at home. I was five, and Jari was twelve when he experienced an unexpected beating. One day, Dad called Jari to the kitchen. He got a drink of water and remained by the sink to keep his distance from our father, whose language was getting heated. I stood behind my mom, clenching her shirt, by the entrance of the kitchen. The screaming grew louder while he pointed his finger into Jari's face. An inch separated the tip of Dad's finger and my brother's nose. The cup hit the floor. Water splashed everywhere. The pokes began. One to his chest, then shoulder, and a body slam against the wall. I don't recall what words Dad yelled, but he had lost control. He grabbed a handful of Jari's blonde locks and hit him several times with his free hand, while his head shook. Jari reached for my dad's grip, keeping his elbows close together, trying to avoid the blows to his face.

My mom tried to intervene from a distance as I stayed behind her, daring to peek at Jari now and then, who had a bloody nose. We didn't exist. Dad ignored Mom, and my cries. I hoped someone would suddenly arrive, and then Dad would stop, and we'd all be safe and happy. What could I do? I wondered: if the police knew about this, how long would it take for them to arrive? They would probably never find us in the woods anyway. We were on our own.

The fight ended by the basement entrance when my dad opened the door and flung Jari down the stairs, then slammed the door shut. On the scuffed-up vinyl floor was a nest of blonde hair. He ordered us to leave him there. I heard my brother tumbling down the splintered wooden staircase, then nothing. *Jari must be dead.* Tears of grief soaked the hem of my mom's shirt. My dad murdered my brother, and everyone would know.

When the coast was clear, against my dad's command, I went downstairs. I had to know if he was still breathing. Slowly I opened the old door, trying not to allow it to creak. I didn't want to see him mangled, laying on the cold concrete, but I mustered up courage and looked down. He was nowhere in sight. The downstairs was dark and dreary with a large furnace on the left, areas for storage and a work area on the right, where my dad would tinker with his chainsaws. Old, cracked cinderblocks formed the walls, which made it freezing. A small window shone some light right where tools lay on a wobbly table. Jari could have escaped out the window and into the night, but where would he go? There were no hospitals, shelters, stores, and no civilian life nearby. If there was, he'd have no explanation for his battered body. He instinctively knew never to expose Dad's rages. The sauna was in the farthest corner of the basement. It was a clean and peaceful space. I could not find Jari anywhere, until I flicked on the light and stepped into the cold sauna. On the top bench, I saw Jari crying with a towel in his hand from the change room. I stared at his face. He had a few scrapes on his forehead and cheeks, a bloodstain on his T-shirt from his nose.

I asked him, "Why was Dad mad at you?"

"I have no idea." he said. I didn't believe him. Jari probably just didn't want to tell me. Dad sometimes behaved like a lunatic, but there must have been a trigger for his rage.

I asked, "Are you ok?" "Yeah." Jari said. I stayed for a few more minutes. I was there for him, not knowing what to do, but I felt a need to be by his side. We just sat there in silence until I sensed he no longer needed me, and then I left. As much as he liked to "torture" his little sis, I wanted to protect him. This incident became an in-home secret between brother and sister.

Sometimes, I wanted Dad to go away. Our home would be peaceful without him, but he was our sole provider, and I would not tattle - even though I thought about it. I thought my voice would not be heard; I didn't matter. But maybe the voice of the operator lady could help; she was a stranger, perhaps she could do something.

Phone operators connected phone calls that were made beyond Kam. She would ask what number was being dialed and connect the caller with the recipient. On the rare occasion that we made a phone call, she was the voice making the connection. All I had to do was pick up the phone, and she would be there, or so I thought. I didn't know that zero had to be dialed first. She was an immediate link to the outside world. Fears flooded my mind about exposing the dark side of our lives, hurting my mom if Dad was forced to leave, and never seeing my dad again. I wanted a dad, I deserved a dad, but I wanted him to stop his madness. The thought of not knowing what the operator lady would do if I told, sealed the vault. Even though I would never tell, her invisible presence gave me an odd sense of comfort.

Chapter 7

## SEVENTY TIMES SEVEN

Anxiety was a normal part of my childhood. Home was as unpredictable as the weather. The forecast wasn't always correct, and it could change at any minute. I learned to go with the flow and merge into whatever the atmosphere was. If anger filled the air, I clenched my teeth. If it was comedy hour, I waited for the giggles to begin. Instability was very much a part of my life. I did my best to predict life, while still just trying to be a kid.

When Dad lay on the couch, snoring like a freight train, the home was calm. But would he wake up as a roaring grizzly or would he be a silly clown? No one could guess. He often wore work trousers with a belt or sometimes suspenders and a flannel button-up shirt. My mom knitted wool socks that he wore all year round. She would mend them when he said, "look, there's a potato sticking out of my sock." On Sundays, for church day, he always wore a suit and tie, and he never had more than stubble on his stern German-looking face. His thin dark hair had a slight wave with a few strands of grey.

## Box of Shame

As much as a house full of screaming kids almost killed his last nerve, he liked children. His grandkids would tease him about his holey socks, and laugh at his sharp toenails bursting through. He would dramatize it by waving around his foot in front of them, wearing only his underwear and socks. The kids would beam with laughter at their silly, silly Pappa. Sometimes he would break out into song and dance on a whim, throwing out a random "Hallelujah" when the mood struck. Other days, we would hear him bellowing through the house, not knowing what set him off.

All of us experienced his anger, but he never laid a hand on Mom. He took out his frustrations on his children, verbally and physically. Both parents grew up with a "spare the rod, spoil the child" mentality; that was their generation. My mom disciplined physically as well, but not often, and she had control. She told me why I'd receive the punishment, and she did not curse or scream. The rare times that I got the whip it was from Mom, and I was glad Dad never thought about doing this. It seemed like he never really thought about discipline. His hands simply reacted out of anger. I preferred Mom's ways. But I once got an unjust punishment that hurt my feelings much more than the slashes of a pussy willow whip. I got a new two-piece winter snowsuit, straight from Zellers, that I loved. The jacket was light grey with a purple corduroy pattern by each shoulder. I loved it because the pattern reminded me of western rodeo attire. I wore it for the season, and then Mom packed it away for the summer. When the snow began to fly the next year, the jacket was lost—vanished into thin air. Mom asked me several times about where I put it. I wish I had an answer, but I could only tell her over and over again, "Mom, I don't know where it is." That year, I had to wear my old winter jacket that I had almost outgrown. A new summer came again, and during a clean-up in the sauna, my mom found the missing jacket. It was under the mattress in the change room. The back was shredded, and part of the internal stuffing was missing. My jaw dropped when she showed it to me, and I assumed Jari must've wrecked it because I loved it, or an animal had got to it. My mom did not believe either of these explanations. Without any facial expression, she asked, "why did you rip the jacket apart?" *What! She thinks I did this?* In disbelief I said, "That was my all-time favorite jacket, and I would never wreck it!" She had heard enough. She walked me outside and told me to get a whip from the bush. I'd learn a lesson about destroying my belongings and telling a lie. Slowly, I walked towards the bush, sniffling as streaks of tears rolled down my cheeks. I held my breath trying to stop them, but the tears flowed. My tears were of disbelief and betrayal that she refused to believe me. I tried to pick a whip that she would be satisfied with; I didn't want her to choose it. There were always lots of pussy willows growing in the spring and early summer. I think she preferred these for punishment because the furry buds can easily be swiped off. I pleaded a few more times for mercy, and she wavered a tad as the discipline ended swiftly. The whip whistled before it hit my hamstrings. I broke free from her grip but not before another slash to my arm. She let me go. My bare skin burned like a row of bees had stung me at the same time. The mystery of the shredded jacket remained unsolved. Our mother/daughter bond broke. It would take time to rebuild trust, but we did.

While Dad was a little on the extreme about most things, Mom had reason. I turned to her for comfort and questions. We could chat about many topics, but not about boys. She married the first one she met, and they married for life. She was a woman of faith in a chaotic marriage, oppressed. I asked her once how many times she would forgive Dad. I learned about the forgiveness of Jesus, but I didn't understand how a person could forgive another for being so hurtful. She said, "God wants us to forgive not only seven times, but seventy times seven. We forgive with our whole heart, just as He has forgiven us. This is what the bible teaches us." I reflected long about her response. Seventy times seven? I had only ten fingers and could not add that high, but it was a whole lot of forgiving. I understood this in the sense that she will put up with him forever, no matter what he does. Tomorrow would be a new day. Perhaps forgiveness would not be necessary.

Marriage, forgiveness, and grown-up things were not my worries. Playtime and farm life were my concerns; the bulls were my friends. They let me sprawl myself on their bellies as they basked in the sunlight. Their sleek shiny coat was a soothing feeling against my skin. Their horns were long, pointy, and could easily kill a human, but they allowed me to join their herd. I'll never forget the sun-baked heat of their hides against my flesh.

Soon I would have less time for farming, when Mom told me I had to go to school just like Jari did. I did not want to leave home, I begged Mom to come with me, but all kids had to go by themselves. Life was so unfair but, if I didn't go, I never would have met the girl I never knew I needed: Pamela.

Chapter 8

# THE FORBIDDEN CLOGS

The bus ride to kindergarten was a great time for a long nap; we could be traveling to another country for all I knew. I put up a huge protest about going to school, at first. I didn't speak English well; it was too far away, and how would I be able to talk to my mom if I needed her? But I did not win the school battle; I was forced to go. My eldest brother was a shy boy and had also fought about going to school, when they moved to Canada. The language barrier was an issue for him as well.

The bus route covered winding, dirt trails and miles of highway travel. The roads could be treacherous in the winters. After what seemed like years of travelling, the bus finally made it to school; I didn't know where I was. I'd never have been able to find my way back, but at least Jari was nearby. The bus driver was a kind young woman who knew Jari and would greet my brother saying, "Good morning, Mr. Smiley." At the end of the day, she'd say, "Goodbye Mr. Smiley, see ya tomorrow." Jari always had that goofy grin on his face, with big dimples that women adored. His golden curls were eye-catching to others, but not to Jari. I was Mr.

Smiley's kid sister, so this would work to my advantage. I hoped that the bus driver would like me as much as she liked my brother.

Not one child in my class spoke Finn, so communicating was a challenge. I was in an environment of rules and forced to sit still while indoors. I felt alone and had to take care of myself; Jari was several grades ahead of me, so I only saw him on the bus. Even though I felt like a scared little kindergartener, I was not alone. All of us were in for new experiences, as we began our education, and I would share this journey with my best friend.

Pamela, a bubbly and happy little girl, stepped onto the bus one morning. She stopped at my seat and said, “Hi, my name’s Pamela. Can I sit with you?” Her soft, blonde hair and bright blue eyes outshone the entire busload of kids. She smiled from ear to ear, for no reason and beamed like a delicate sunflower. *What was she so happy about anyway?* I liked her, and we had an instant connection. Pamela made me her friend, and we sat right behind the bus driver every day. After kindergarten, space at a nearby school became available, and many of the neighborhood children transferred closer to home. The bus rides were shorter, and sometimes I rode my bike to school, which was a few miles away on the winding dirt roads. Jari told me we would be attending McDonald's School. I was excited!

"We get to have lunch there every day?" I asked.

"Yup!" Jari smiled.

"We can have McNuggets and sundaes for lunch?" This is the best school ever, I thought.

"Definitely."

The first day at our new school arrived, and there weren't any golden arches. The school was called MacDonald Public School, not McDonald's like the restaurant, but what did I know at that age? Jari's tricks fooled me again. I was gullible, and he could almost make me believe anything. I once saw the words, "Antiques for Sale," in the window of a store. I asked my big brother what "anti-ques" meant. He said, "it means Q-tips stupid. They sell Q-tips." Imagine that! An entire store full of Q-tips! He was so mean, and I fell for his pranks every time.

The school was awesome even without the McNuggets and sundaes. Just as Jari deceived me into thinking that I was going to McDonalds for school, I did the same to others. Most did not believe me, but if Mom was nearby, she would confirm the name of my school, then I'd laugh and say, "See, I do go to McDonalds school!" They probably thought I was the luckiest kid on earth.

The school sat in the middle of the bush. Natures bushes and trees fenced us in. Gravel roads were nearby, and transport trucks could faintly be heard from the distant highway. Our only caution came in the spring, when the black bears would emerge hungry from hibernation.

My teacher was kind-hearted, and I loved her. I had friends and thought I would graduate from this school, but fate would prove otherwise. After only three years at the school, it caught fire one evening and quickly burned out of control, leaving only ash and rubble behind - a new school would be too costly. Rumors of arson began to grow in the neighborhood before the investigation was complete. The inspection had no solid answers, but the fire likely started in the furnace and electrical room. Where would I go to school now? Just as I became comfortable with school life, it disappeared. We missed a small part of our education, while we waited to be transferred to another community for the remainder of grade three. The bus rides were once again long and boring, but I had Pam next to me.

Pam and I grew close and had a lot in common. We were both blonde, blue-eyed girls with Finnish heritage; although, she had some Ukrainian blood in her as well. We both loved the outdoors, art and attended church. Years later, we learned that our home lives had some commonalities as well, such as having no toilet in the house. Being different from other kids was something we kept to ourselves, because we didn't want to feel like the weird kids. We shared a few shenanigans in our next school, as besties do. Pineview Public school, along the trans-Canada highway, had about ninety students. The building had no gymnasium, so a school bus took us to a bigger school down the highway for gym class twice a week.

During gym, one day, I brought two pairs of fashionable, wooden clogs that came from Finland, to school. One pair was red, with a Dutch clog appearance, and the other had a pointier toe, tan leather, and a flowery vine pattern etched into it. Pam fell in love with them, and we wanted to wear them on the bus trip to gym class, even though our teacher said we had to wear our winter boots. We were disappointed. Everyone would be envious of the clogs, so we just *had* to wear them, but getting by the teacher would be tricky. Somehow, we managed to sneak them past her onto the bus, and we were off to the other school. In the change room, we put them in our bags so we would not get caught. A flawless plan. We thought we were so clever.

After class, our classmates got dressed in their jackets and footwear. With our clogs hiding in our bags, we stood still, not knowing what to do next. We didn't dare take them out. Mrs. Sifton, our teacher, said, "Hurry up girls, get your boots on." We looked at each other, with dread and fear.

"We don't have them," I said.

"Why not?" Replied Mrs. Sifton.

Pam offered an explanation, "Maybe someone stole them."

"Well, we better ask if anyone has seen them. Perhaps someone borrowed them."

My palms were getting sweaty, and a knot of some sort built up in my throat as I tried to gulp. I was hoping to just stand there, and Mrs. Sifton would ask around on our behalf, but that is not what happened. Instead, she made us knock on each classroom door, interrupting the lesson, to ask if anyone had seen our boots. We each gave a detailed description of what they looked like, but sure enough, no one had seen them. I felt so guilty about wasting everyone's time about our stupid boots when I knew exactly where they were.

In Sunday school, we learned about the lying snowball. Tell the truth from the start, before one lie turns into a gigantic snowball, out of control. I was now trapped in the middle of it, if only I'd been truthful from the beginning. The bus was loaded with the students growing impatient, while we continued to search for our imaginary boots. After the long search was over, Mrs. Sifton allowed us to wear our indoor gym shoes onto the bus. The fifteen-minute bus ride was not enough time to make another plan. We shuffled in our seats, whispering about how much trouble we would be in. *Now I hoped that our boots really were stolen.*

The bus arrived at our home school, and we all walked inside towards the coatroom, and there, sitting on the rack, were two pairs of girl's boots. After the coatroom was clear, I stood there dumbfounded. I looked at Mrs. Sifton with a half-grin, sad puppy eyes and said, "How did those get there?" *She can't be mad at a puppy, can she?* We were busted! Mrs. Sifton stood there in a pretty, striped blouse, with her hands on her hips. She stomped her high heeled boot, firmly onto the floor, as she demanded to see our bags. Sheepishly, we unzipped our duffle bags, and she saw the forbidden clogs. Her glaring eyes stared into mine, and my lips sealed tight; I'd never seen this side of her. There wasn't a lecture, and she didn't ask questions, as her only words were, "To the office, NOW!"

Our teacher was disappointed in us, and it didn't feel good. Both of us understood right from wrong. My defiant streak was stronger than Pam's, but she always sat in my corner. Upsetting our favorite teacher, and facing the principal's wrath, felt like the end of the world. Only bad kids were sent to the office. The principal gave his lecture, and saw that we were on the verge of tears, so he let us off with a warning. I thought being sent to the principal's office was the most terrifying moment in life, but then I learned what fear was.

Chapter 9

# WHERE THE BAD GUYS LIVE

On Sundays, Mom would pack a heap of food for my dad's week in the bush. He always had Ruisleipä (Finnish Rye bread), pulla (cardamom sweet coffee bread), a variety of meats, along with a sack of potatoes and carrots from the garden. We would stay home and wait for him to return. Dad was a bush contractor back in the day when only basic equipment was used. Machines were not computerized, air-conditioned, or have satellite radios. The operator's cab was window-free, so the black flies would swarm my dad in a feeding frenzy, and there was no escape from the dusty, stagnant air. The workday was hard labor, and only men with bull strength and Sisu could do it successfully. (Sisu is a word used by Finns to describe courage, strength, and perseverance. An inner toughness found within.) Dad would be stationed in the bush with his home-made trailer, along with other laborers close by, for the week. The trailer had two single beds, a miniature table separating them, a few old banged-up metal kitchen cupboards with a sink, but no running water. He kept his food in a cooler with ice. A small wooden stove heated the 10 x 16-foot space. Dad used a

Coleman propane cooking element to cook on, which once blew up in his face, singed off his facial hairs, and melted a layer of skin. He was on bed rest for weeks, bandaged up, and he looked awful. My sister Marja tended to his wounds because he protested going to the hospital, even though she insisted. Dad refused and believed that he would be healed with her help, and sure enough, bush life was calling his name in no time. He loved the sanctity, peacefulness of the isolation, and the satisfaction of a hard day's work.

Marja became the first registered nurse of the family and relocated to Toronto shortly after graduating from nursing school. She flew home to care for Dad; she washed his face, applied a nasty-smelling ointment, and changed the dressings daily. She was the second oldest of the clan. Marja had a unique style in clothing and skipped makeup, except for lipstick. Her beauty came naturally; she was one classy lady. While most of us kids had various shades of blonde hair, hers was quite dark, and she curled it with rollers. She was a striking woman. She traveled the world and helped with my travel expenses, to visit her in Toronto.

My dad's work took him to different forestry sectors in the region. Contracts would end, and he would search for another, which wasn't difficult to do. Dad had an excellent reputation as a worker, and he had no fears about talking to anybody that would listen; people loved him. Sometimes he would explore bush roads and cutting areas where there could be potential for upcoming work, and I would come along. Ritchie also came with us at times. We would have a packed lunch and pick blueberries if we saw them. Blueberry picking was a common family trip taken often, and Mom made the best blueberry pies.

When it was just Ritchie and I, Dad would race through the bush roads. He would let us sit in the box of the truck, on top of the green wooden homemade toolbox, on our knees. Our tummies pressed against the back window, arms stretched out on the roof, pretending to steer our imaginary steering wheels. The wind and dust would hit my face, and my long hair would tousle behind me.

"Woooo hoooo Ritchie, we are flying!"

Ritchie's white T-shirt flapped on his sides. "Yeah, this is awesome!"

Dad kept his eye on us from the rear-view mirror and would quickly notice if a body went missing. The ride was noisy, bumpy, and we were engulfed in a big dust cloud, but Ritchie and I continued *driving* our trucks.

"Look at me Ritchie, I'm going faster than you!"

Ritchie would pretend to stomp on the pedal with full sound effects and yell, "not for long, sucker!" We would burst into laughter, loving my dad's speeding.

When the ride got too jarring, we'd have to drop our *steering wheels* and latch onto the lip of the toolbox, to prevent ourselves from flying overboard. The truck was a plain half-ton without lights or bars on the roof to hang onto. We were thrilled and having the ride of our lives, but we knew if our moms were there, we would not be allowed near the roof of the truck.

During the weekdays when Dad was gone, Mom held down the fort, which was exactly what I preferred. I could watch whatever I wanted on TV, without Dad yanking the cord out whenever he entered the living room, and I knew the house would be calm. Mom played games with me and read me Finnish stories from my bookshelf. I took dad's place in the bed, when he wasn't there, and enjoyed the warmth of my moms' body. In a fetal position under the covers, I'd have a restful sleep, loved and secure. "I love you, Mom," I'd whisper." Puss, my warm and cuddly tomcat, would be curled up in a ball at the foot of the bed. I named him after the story, Puss in Boots.

Sometimes the weeks dragged on without Dad's transportation but going to the city was not impossible. Occasionally, neighbors would offer rides, but most times, we would manage on our own. Town ventures were a treat, especially the way we traveled. Our home was less than a mile from the main highway, where the Grey Goose Bus Lines would travel. The bus went throughout Canada traveling from coast to coast, and we didn't need pre-purchased tickets. A simple wave at the bus or a thumbs up, would bring the bus to a halt.

We waited on the side of the highway, and when Mom saw the bus approaching, she flagged down the driver. Nods and smiles were exchanged as she handed the driver some coins. The passing trees whizzed by, and the speeding traffic was an amazing sight from the huge window of the bus. This felt like a luxury, sailing down the paved road in a smooth, quiet ride. The cushions are as soft as comfy clouds, with a criss-cross pattern, and the seats had a slight recline. I felt like royalty in this house on wheels.

The bus brought us into the downtown area, and we had all day in town before we would catch another travel bus to get home. There was a nice mall near the waterfront and plenty of restaurants to choose from. The Eaton's building is the fancy store where we mostly window shopped. The enormous center had three levels. The escalator brought us to the fine China and candy store. Sometimes Mom would buy me treats for the ride back. In December, it would turn into a spectacular Christmas dreamland. Wherever we wanted to go in town, we would get there by foot. Mom didn't know how to read the bus routes, and the transfers confused her. A taxi may have been an option, but they were too pricey, and I sensed she didn't trust being in a car with a strange man. She loved the outdoors and walking, so that was never an issue – until one day it was.

I had just finished grade four and was looking forward to a carefree summer. On a beautiful, sunny afternoon in the city, Mom and I were walking in a quiet neighborhood heading to her friend's place; we had time to kill. Mom was wearing her usual outfit: a long grey dress jacket tied at the waist and black dress shoes with a low heel. She always kept her hair short and permed. She didn't like to fuss over her appearance. There was not one vain cell in her body, but she always looked nice on town trips. We were passing respectable houses in a middle-class neighborhood, coming up to a stop sign just down the hill. The street was a one-way route, and every house had a front lawn and a driveway to park in. We'd often walked this street before. The afternoon was quiet with no traffic nearby.

I begin to hear footsteps behind us. The sounds of the *clippety-clop* noise of a horse's hooves. *I hope I'm hearing horses, but I know they don't live in the city.* I sneak a quick peek and see two young men, with long bushy hair, bell-bottom jeans, and clunky platform heels, like the disco shoes. They are strolling on the street a few houses back. We are on the sidewalk now, going a little faster. Mom squeezes my hand tighter, but says nothing, and we continue walking. I am content and unaware of the impending danger.

Suddenly, thundering clacks from the disco shoes are sprinting towards us. Mom yanked my arm, practically dislocating my shoulder, and screamed, "Juokse! Juokse!" We took off running from the bad guys. I glanced over my shoulder, and the two guys were catching up to us. My feet couldn't keep up with my body, which was forced forward by my mom. *This was bad news. I should have stayed home where it was safe, sleeping with the 500 lb. bulls.* The men caught up to us and tried to snatch my mom's sand-coloured purse. She fought back, yelled and flailed her arms about.

*I must do something! What?* My body won't move. I can't piece together what is happening. I am only a few feet away, behind my mom, and I can't breathe. One man tries to secure my mom's arm back, while the other man struggles with her purse. *Do they have a gun? Will they kill her? Men like these only lived under my bed. This must be a dream.* In terror, I thought to myself, they might kidnap me, and I'll never see my mom again. My face would be the first milk carton kid to appear in Canada. Children would stare at me every morning while they ate their cereal. I would be lost forever. These guys need a taste of my dad's anger, and I wished he would suddenly appear, so the punks would run for their lives.

The fight seems to go on for hours, but it's probably only minutes, and with one more powerful tug, the thieves win. They run down the hill, with my four-and-a-half-foot mom on their tail. She chases them, while yelling to a stranger who is watering his lawn, "Poliisi, Poliisi!" I see the man drop his garden hose and sprint to his door; I don't remember if the police ever came. Suddenly, I am free to run, and I race towards my mom. My feet moved so fast, I'm sure they don't even touch the asphalt. Once I gain momentum, I run like I do in my dreams, full speed ahead with each elongated step. Each thrust of my little legs moves me miles ahead. The men veer off into a hidden over-grown laneway and my mom stops at the end of the street. The thugs escape with her purse, but Mom and I are alive and unharmed.

I got a glimpse of darkness in the world. City people could be dangerous. My mom was a generous woman, so it was hard to believe that other people were not, and they would steal from her while she walked with her young daughter. When I grew up, I planned to find those bad guys, force them to pay back every penny they stole and make them apologize for attacking us.

Chapter 10

# HORSING AROUND

I never wanted to live in the city; I loved the country. The incident shook my faith in humankind. My mom was my protector, and I felt assured in her presence. Still, the bad guys found us. I prayed we'd never experience that again.

Our neighborhood was quiet and meeting up with thugs like that, was never a concern. We had a few neighbors within miles of us who became friends. We country folks watched out for each other. My brother's buddies were nearby, but Pam and a few others lived far away until a young Finnish family moved in just down the road from us. Johanna was my age, and she was the eldest of three children. Her mother was a stay-at-home mom like mine, and all of us spoke Finnish. The walk from my house to hers was only about fifteen minutes, but it was even less by cutting through the neighbor's field.

I loved Johanna's free and fun-loving spirit, and she cracked me up with her wild sense of humor. She was a sandy blonde and several inches taller than me. She liked to show off her double-jointed knuckles by naturally bending the top part of her fingers, saying that it was a rare trait to have. I could only do it by forcing my joints in place with my other hand. We became inseparable, sharing many laughs and sleepovers at each other's houses, and I trusted her completely.

Johanna and I had no fear of swimming in the pond with the big-lipped bottom feeders. We dove for clay to create our art, enjoyed styling our hair and buying matching outfits for school. Together we were team *girl power.* We were fearless and would stand against Jari and his friends. We made our own rules, and were total weirdos! Johanna and I knew most of the Kamlanders within biking distance. Close to our houses was a white shack with a rainbow painted on the side of one wall. We rode our banana bikes by this dwelling many times, assessing the property. The only occupants were the owner and his dogs. He didn't seem like a family man, but we were curious about the loner and wanted to visit him. We both had a bit of hesitation.

After weeks of discussion about whether a serial killer lived in our neighborhood, we made contact. He looked like he'd just stepped out of the 60s with his Grizzly Adams beard and a sash around his waist. He was soft-spoken, gentle, and an artist like us. Eventually, we went into the house to see his artwork which he displayed around his living room. There were several stained-glass designs and some paintings. We satisfied our curiosity; our neighbor was not a murderer. I would always have Johanna join me in my adventures. Country life was beautiful, predators existed, but not in our community.

Our summers were long and amazing, and we created school projects before school even began. The teacher selections were probably not chosen yet, but our excitement about going into grade five bubbled over. We decided to create a project about Finland. We researched Finnish culture from my new stack of encyclopedias and added a personal touch by discussing life in the good old days. Our parents told us about traditional customs, farm living, and poverty, before they immigrated to Canada.

On the first day of school, we brought our creation with us. Our folder held pages of written information, pictures, and drawings. Johanna's mom had to drive us to school on the first day, because we had large Bristol boards of maps and illustrations; lugging our work onto the bus would've been impossible. A grade wasn't given, but we didn't care, we were thrilled to show off our hard work to the teacher. She was surprised! She hung our board up on the wall so that students could learn about Finnish culture, thanks to Johanna and me. We were proud of our project.

The summer after grade five ended, we got exciting news. Johanna's family were getting horses; our lifelong dreams were coming true. When Johanna called to tell me, I had my doubts, but her dad confirmed it was true. I would be involved in all horse matters because her family accepted me as one of their own. I was obsessed with horses. I was mesmerized by their beautiful strong bodies and flowing manes. I asked my parents for a horse, since my mom had told me that country folks always had horses in Finland; but they were not for pleasure; their purpose was for field work and transportation. She said, "horses require a lot of work and money and are no longer a necessity in this day and age." I knew she was right about the money.

One spring, Dad made another trip to his homeland in Finland. Since arriving in Canada in 1960, he'd traveled there a few times to see his family. On this trip, he told me he would bring back a horse for me. Johanna was getting horses, and I too was going to get a horse. Doubts still crossed my mind though. He must've meant that he would buy me a horse when he returned from his trip. Shipping livestock from Europe to Canada didn't seem realistic. Would he actually do that? Mom would never allow it, as it would cost a fortune. Perhaps he was referring to a barbie horse with the real manes, tails, and saddles, just in case I started to prepare for a horse.

I hunted for fence posts in the wood piles scattered around the yard and scoured the woods for a good, sturdy fallen tree, that I could cut and drag towards the house. Not far from the house was a dead limb, with only a few branches left on it. I worked for days using a rusty old saw and ax, to create a point at one end, then dug a hole as deep as possible into the earth. I plopped the five-foot log onto the ground and pushed the clay and dirt around to secure it. The post wobbled quite a bit, so I gave it a couple more good stomps into the base and figured it will be sturdy enough once it all settled; one post in, only a thousand more to go. I couldn't help but be excited when Dad got home. He unpacked his belongings, and I waited for a response, sitting in front of the boob tube pretending to ignore him. Dad came into the living room and said, "Here's your horse." In his hand, he held a clear glass horse figurine with a deep blue marble effect on the inside, a household decoration.

The spark of hope I held for him disappeared. I thanked him but wondered what thoughts bounced around his brain. Could it be a thoughtful gift from father to daughter? Was it a mean joke? Maybe my dad knew about the upcoming horses from Johanna's dad, and maybe they talked about it. I was a little disappointed, but I didn't waste much time thinking about it. Johanna and I had to prepare for the horses.

We had many sleepless nights, full of giggles, as we talked about how our lives would change and the adventures we would have. We studied everything about horses. We both had artistic talent, and we drew amazing horse pictures that we hung all over our walls. We subscribed to Horse Illustrated and read each word about their care, including hoof trimming, diet, and barrel racing. While we planned out our rides and horse care, Johanna's dad built a small barn and fenced in their property.

Champion arrived first. He was a retired 13-year-old Standardbred harness racing horse. A handsome brown fellow with a black mane, tail, and hocks. Shortly after, from the same pasture, came Bingo and Future – a mom and daughter. They were a two-for-one deal, as they were neglected ponies, saved from the dog meat factory. We suspected animal abuse because Future's black body shivered from human touch, and her coat was a dull, matted mess. Bingo was a brown and white Shetland pony, with missing patches of fur and snapped at everyone who approached her. Both needed love and patience, especially Future.

Life had never been so fabulous. I enjoyed taking care of them – everything from riding and grooming, to scooping out their manure from the barn. I loved every stinky minute of it! While Johanna's two siblings complained about the stench, I jumped into my rubber boots to muck the barn. The foul smell reminded me that my life revolved around horses, and I was the luckiest cowgirl on earth. Two friends worked as a team to feed them, style their manes, keep their home clean, and most of all, love them. One winter, instead of a food fight, we had a manure fight. As soon as it started flying in the air, Johanna's little sister ran out screaming bloody murder, as we pelted each other with handfuls of frozen horse crap, laughing uncontrollably. Neither of our moms were impressed with the laundry that week.

Although the horses were not living at my house, I felt like they were mine - I shared the workload. Two more horses joined the family later, Cinnamon and Blaze. Cinnamon was part Quarter horse and had one blue eye and one brown. She was lovely and somehow Johanna created the nickname,

"Un-Bun" for me, based on Cinnamon. "Cinna-mon and Un-Bun," it was a combination she liked to say, and the name stuck for decades; although, sometimes I was called Un for short. Blaze was an eighteen-year-old solid, brown horse which belonged to Johanna's mom's friend. The friend was moving and needed to find a home for Blaze. He was well-trained and fit in perfectly with the horse family, but because of his age, he spent more time in the field than on the trails.

Once Future grew to trust our gentle hands, it would be my job to train her to allow riders on her back, then I could call her my own. The process was slow, but eventually she cooperated with the training. The day finally arrived when I could sit on her back, and I was excited! Soon we would gallop down the road, and I was anxious to feel her strides. Champion was a trotter by nature, and it was a bumpy ride. Cinnamon was the perfect rocking horse, smooth, and she never missed a beat. Now it was time to discover Future's gait.

Johanna's dad held her by the bridle so she wouldn't bite me and helped me climb up. She accepted me, and he led us around the yard to ensure Future was comfortable with a rider, then he handed me the reins. It was just Future and me. I kept her at a slow walk, as she'd never been ridden before, and she had to learn that I was in charge of which direction we would go. My patience and love paid off. Future responded to every command I gave her, as we strolled around the garage, until she had enough and bucked me off. I tumbled to the ground, scraped my hands on the gravel, feeling like she'd always be feral, and I'd failed as a trainer. I thought we had this amazing horse-to-human bond, but Future needed more time to build trust.

I whisked the sand away from my pants and said, "I'm going inside." I was frustrated and too scared to try again. Horse training was a lot harder than I thought. Johanna's dad made me get back on, saying, "when you fall off the saddle, you dust yourself off and climb back on;" those words stuck with me. He encouraged me not to give up, so I had to show him my brave side. Even though being kicked or stomped on was a risk, I would not disappoint him. That day I learned that I was tougher than I realized.

Aside from the horses, I still looked forward to town trips, especially with Johanna. We did less walking on the streets, and Mom no longer carried a purse. The hustle and bustle of the city became a pleasant change of scenery. On weekends, when Dad was home, we would head to the city in our 1972 grey Chevy half-ton. Mom never got a license, so we depended on Dad for transportation. Sometimes neighbors would hitch a ride with us, and there could be six people sitting on top of each other without seat belts; rules were lenient. Groceries and banking were our main errands, then back-to-school shopping, which was a big deal. Pencils, binders, and new outfits were a must.

Sunday was a day of rest; stores were closed so that business owners could rest as well. We always attended Sunday morning church, often followed by lunch in a restaurant - Dad loved eating out, especially buffets. My parents were founders of the church I grew up in. They began this journey in the homes of fellow believers in the early 1960s. My dad was familiar with living-room-style church meetings from his childhood, and he followed in his dad's footsteps by preaching in private homes. My parents were active within the local Finnish community and formed friendships with other Christians.

My dad and a few friends created a board and eventually decided to become registered as a church. This would allow for some funding, and no one would be turned away due to lack of space. Guest speakers traveled from Finland, Canada, and the United States to visit the Finnish Free Church (Vappaakirkko). Eventually, a permanent pastor was found, and the church flourished. Mom and Dad remained active members of the little, yellow church on John Street for the rest of their lives. When I was twelve, my mom was excited to tell the church ladies a remarkable story about a visitor I had. Some believed in supernatural experiences, while others were skeptical. My mom knew the truth, and that's all that mattered.

Chapter 11

# THE VISION

Within five years after arriving in Kam, we built a beautiful home that sat on top of a hill across the road from the farmhouse. A new family purchased our farmhouse, followed by several other families that came and went. Peace and quiet drew them to nature, but the everlasting renovations turned them away. A money pit not worth their time and effort. Finally, a nice couple moved in with their teenage daughter, and they made the home their own. The neighbors had no plans for livestock, so they allowed us to play in the empty barn. We'd climb up the stacked hay bales, that almost reached the roof, and swing from one end to the other. The property was fenced in from when we had the bulls there, so they let us bring the horses to the field to graze. The herd loved the change in pasture and would race up and down the hills, whinnying and passing gas in excitement. They'd reach the top of the hill where we stood and kick their heels to the blue sky. Cinnamon was the most playful one, like a toddler with bounds of energy. My ears still hear the thunder, and the vibrations of racing hooves are still felt beneath my feet. The closer the horses came, the stronger the rumbling felt. We would laugh hysterically as they galloped and performed.

Our new home was spacious with a large living room and solid rust-colored carpeting. The farthest wall had the greatest wallpaper I'd ever seen. It was a life-sized walking trail through a forest, with birch trees standing tall on either side of the path. Our property was full of trees and trails to roam but bringing the forest into our living room was epic! Every time I entered the living room, I imagined going down the path to an open field of horses. The wall was a welcoming focal point in the home. There was a lovely patio with a fantastic view of the red barn, hills of grass, and the sauna by the pond. The long hallway had three doors, all of which were bedrooms. One for my parents, another for Jari, and for the first time, I had my own room – with light pink walls. There was a bathroom at the end of the hall with a flushing toilet. Jari could no longer bang the flimsy sides of the outhouse to scare me. It was a real washroom with an actual door.

Jari did not live in the house for long. He wanted a part-time job, so he moved to town and stayed with Niina and her husband. I was on my own in my dream home, no more musty smells, just the smell of fresh paint. Fuzzy insulation in the walls kept the house warm and toasty, and the downstairs had plenty of room with a play area in the corner, opposite the large wood-burning furnace by the indoor sauna. I never wanted to leave and had plans to live there after my parents could no longer care for the home.

When I was twelve, a vision came to me. I was certain I was taken out of my bed at night and placed into a different dimension. Could this have been an out-of-body experience? There is no logical way to explain this. All I knew was that it happened. Life was as normal as could be. I went to bed, thanked God for the horses, my mom, and my home. I asked for a new bike but instead, I received a hug from Jesus.

I see myself asleep on our velvety plush couch. It's a royal burgundy color, and the sun shines through the big bay window. The beaming light is bright and warm; my eyes open as the brightness intensifies to an unnatural level. I squint while rising from the sofa. A figure stands by the patio door, enveloped in the intense illumination. It is Jesus. Not a single doubt enters my mind. I push myself up with my mouth ajar and in a few steps, I am before Him. He hugs me and a comforting power, surges through my body, and joyful tears stream down my cheeks. I'd never experienced this emotion in my material world. The surge intensifies. I am not afraid. I ask him, “Am I coming with you?” He says, “Now is not your time.” I close my eyes tight, still in his embrace, and as the light fades and the trembling slows, I open my eyes and find myself in my mom’s arms for a fleeting moment before she morphs into a smoky figure and vanishes. I am alone in the living room, by the patio door. My arms are empty.

In the morning, I bounce out of bed and run to speak with my mom to see what she remembers from yesterday. I’m overflowing with joy but still extremely confused. She listens intently, captivated by my words, as I describe what happened. She believes in Jesus, Heaven, and angels. This is a familiar story to her, and she needs to know the details. “What did he say next? Did you want to go with him?” She had been through a similar experience with my sister, prior to my birth. My late sister told my mom that she had been playing with angels in the closet. A few days later, the angels came again and took her home to be with Jesus. She was hit by a car at age five, was in a coma for a few days, and never regained consciousness.

Mom reached for a pen and paper and jotted down some notes, as we sat at the kitchen table chatting. She wanted a record of this. She said, “I wasn't there. That was between you and Jesus." She didn't know why he visited me, but I received a magnificent gift. I was certain she was there, the three of us. I had no explanation but knew I would never forget this experience of complete love and peace. Jesus hugged me in my living room and spoke to me. *Was it at night? During the day? How does the existence of time and the clock on the wall differ from earth and Heaven?* I didn't know. I only knew I met Him. I don't know why this gift was given to me, but I was satisfied that Mom believed me. Most people would simply call this a dream, which I know for sure it was not. I waited and waited for Jesus to return, often laying on the couch where I first met Him, but He never came back. There were unanswered questions. Why did He come? Would he take my parents? And Puss? He left too soon, and I didn't get answers. I had to stop looking for Him and just accept that I would see Him again whenever my time is up. Did He come to offer comfort? Or to remind me I will be in complete safety one day? I didn't need to see Him physically move a mountain. He appeared before me and squeezed me tight in his arms. The incredible event left me baffled, and it was too inconceivable to share with my friends. Who would believe me? I was blessed by His presence and felt special, and someone else thought I was special too.

Chapter 12

## RONNIE

Our home was open to family, friends, and strangers. Considering the distance from town, where many of our family and friends lived, we had a lot of visitors pass through. We always had enough food and space to share. Some people came and went, while others stayed longer. During one of these visits, we had a guest stay over for the weekend who became a friend. Jari had left for town life, so I had company.

Ronnie lived in foster care. Our former neighbors hired him for yard work on occasion, so he'd been in the area before. His father landed in prison when Ronnie was three, so both he and his sister were put in foster care, as their mom was unable to provide for them. He stayed with us for an extended weekend get-away from his foster family, who unfortunately appeared to enjoy the monthly pay cheques they received, more than Ronnie's company. We shared our country life with him and gave him a change of scenery.

His hair was thin, wispy, and dark like his eyes. When he talked, he tucked his hair behind his ears. A golden snake pendant sometimes fell on top of his T-shirt. Although still a teenager, his teeth had a hint of yellow. I could not explain the slight bit of uneasiness I felt around him, but my curiosity only drew me closer to him. Everyone liked his friendliness, including me, but he tended to shy away from direct eye contact. Quickly we became friends, while I took him fishing in the pond for suckerfish and showed him the horses. We sat on the small dock reminiscing like an old married couple, but we'd only just met.

"Your life is really cool; I wish I didn't have to leave soon; I love hanging out with you." The flattery was getting him everywhere. *A teenager thought I was cool!* A little girl crush is normal in the pre-teen stage.

"Aw, I like being with you too, Ronnie." My cheeks blushed, and butterflies fluttered about in my tummy.

A few hours of laughs and adventures had passed, and I somehow ended up on Ronnie's side of a secret plan, without even knowing it. My young impressionable mind surrendered to his advances of secret hugging and smooching. This territory reminded me of kissing tag that I had played at school. I liked to get a kiss from some boys, but I would run for my life from others, so I didn't get tagged. I would let Ronnie tag me, but it was rather risky when he came into the sauna change room for hugs and cuddles.

The sauna was down the hill from the house. We had one inside our house, and another outdoor one, by the pond. The bathing area was large enough for several people, and the change room had a separate door and windows. There was a bed, dresser, and a couch. My eldest brother and his young family lived there for a short time between house moves. The muddy pond was close by, and I always changed into my bathing suit there before swimming in the pond. I expected Ronnie to meet me at the dock, but he entered the change room area just as I gathered some towels from the shelf to take to the watering hole. Ronnie playfully pushed me onto the bed, landing on top of me.

"Hey, what are you doing?" I blurted in surprise.

"Cuddling with my girl." Ronnie lay on his side, resting his head on his palm, while his other arm crossed my body at my waist. Softly, he smiled, and I began to relax and enjoy an intimate moment with him. Ronnie kissed my cheek and then whispered lovely words to me.

"You're such a beautiful woman."

*A woman? Me? Really? Why yes, I am a woman. I did what I damn well wanted. I had a training bra and caught the attention of a teen, and we flirted a lot.* Tenderly he brushed my hair off my shoulder and gently caressed my arm.

"Thanks, you make me feel that way." I didn't know what to say. *Did I sound like a dork?*

Awkwardness crept in. He saw me as a woman, and I tried to portray one. With Ronnie near, I was special; a male showered me with attention, and I enjoyed it. My mom was in the house preparing supper, and Dad's chainsaw revved up in the bush as he cut firewood.

We were alone; Ronnie wiggled closer to my body and asked, "Do you wanna try sex?"

Doing *it* never crossed my mind. Kissing a boy pushed the boundaries, but sex was for marriage; this was a value I'd been taught. But because Ronnie suggested it, the thought crossed my mind. With a slight bit of hesitation, I said, "I've never done it, and it will hurt." Ronnie, being a little older, convinced me that he would be gentle, and it would be almost painless. "This is not a safe place either. If my parents found us, we'd be dead meat." My curiosity about the whole idea dwindled, but I didn't want him to stop liking me.

"We would hear footsteps coming up the stairs before the squeaky old door would open," he said. "Don't worry honey; you're safe with me."

I was being lured in, trusting his wisdom and words. He was mature and seemed intelligent, like he knew a thing or two. Soon he would be flying the coop and starting his life, and I could be by his side. My heart melted, all morals and values that I had slowly dissipated into space, and I was thoroughly powerless, without even knowing it. *Duped.* Blindly, I walked a path away from my innocent childhood to a world I could never return from.

I never once imagined Ronnie would hurt me, but his powers were invisible. The more we moved beyond the hugging stage, the more uncomfortable I grew, but he led the way, and I followed like a lamb to slaughter. Ronnie gently gave direction and guided my moves. He threw the floral orange sheet over us on the bed and told me to take my bathing suit off. A body lay on top of me, my pale skin against his light brown reflection, and I couldn't see an escape as the word "no" started to form on my lips. I don't know why, but I'd lost my power, my will, and I continued trusting his judgment.

Without warning, a clattering sound came from the sauna stove. “What’s that?!” I quietly shrieked, as I pushed him away and leaped into my bathing suit, like it was a magic trick. Ronnie pulled up his shorts, jumped off the bed, and stood close to the door. I listened for a few seconds and realized that my mom was outside adding logs to the woodstove. I had a list of excuses as to why Ronnie and I were in the change room and hoped that she would fall for one of them. The noise stopped, and I waited for her to enter the change room. I peeked between the window curtains and saw her walking up towards the house. *Relief.* She came to stoke the fire. This disruption had to be a sign, and I found the courage to say no. As smitten and infatuated as I was, I needed it to end before I lost my innocence. I realized this was wrong, and I didn’t want to lose my virginity.

“Close call, but she doesn’t know we’re in here.” Ronnie took me by the hand and brought me to the bed.

“Ronnie, I don’t think we should do this.” I hesitated and hoped he’d see it my way, but he insisted that we continue.

He was smooth and sly, and I don’t know how I found myself laying under the sheets again, as he helped to take off my bathing suit. His coaxing continued, and with every passing second, I hoped he would stop, but he didn't. My mind remained stuck on the possibility that my mom might come back at any moment. If my dad walked in, Ronnie better run for his life, while I die of shame. Physically it was almost impossible and very awkward. I got through it just as Ronnie said, with only a little pain. *I'm sure he really loves me now. We are meant to be.* The deed was done; I made love - I was initiated into womanhood at age twelve.

The next day, we both remained cool, as if nothing had happened. He had one more day with us, and then I didn't know if I'd ever see him again. We talked about how he would come to work for my dad or a neighbor. Ronnie would find some way to get back to me; he had to - we had a special bond. He left the following day, and I was crushed. The next week at school, I had to tell someone. I told Johanna first and then Pam. They couldn't believe that it had gone that far. My mind was in a state of denial, and I could not recognize that Ronnie had done something unforgivable.

I daydreamed, doodling Ronnie's name on my hand with a heart around it. I was head-over-heals, and I thought about him constantly. We were united by our physical act of love. It placed me into a unique category from others. I was different, a grown-up, and I was under his spell. The subtle sense of shame lurking in the background was quickly eliminated by telling myself *I, Anita, a beautiful woman, made an adult decision all by myself. I should be proud.*

Within a week or so after he left, my feelings flipped to disgust. It felt like a thick curtain was drawn, and my peaceful scenery disappeared. My new world was a dismal existence of darkness, one that I should never live in. My feelings of love suddenly got replaced with shame, humiliation, and confusion set in. This came out of nowhere and hit my heart like thunder. Self-hate, disgust, and shame consumed me. Prayer and repentance would not free me from my sins, nothing could help. I deserved invisible punishment. My shattered heart wept in pain from a deep desecration of a sexual violation against my soul. There was no fixing this. I could not reach inside my body and take it out. It was there to stay; this secret found its home in me.

I wanted Ronnie to die! The pain tortured me, and these feelings could not be erased in the shower. Every morning I'd wake up to the same gut-wrenching ache that was eating me alive from the inside out. I was trapped and had to do anything possible to release myself from these feelings. My diary and Puss in Boots, heard all about my revulsion for Ronnie, and I prayed for cleansing. I was dirty; my parents would not approve and would not love me anymore. My dad would face jail time for blowing Ronnie's parts off, and I would be to blame. The confusion over my deep shame made no sense at all, and if I did have someone to talk to, I would not be able to find the words to describe how I felt.

I kept my mouth shut and only allowed a secret inner chaos. When either of the girls asked if I'd heard from Ronnie, I cringed at hearing his name but pretended like we were growing apart. I could never reveal the wounded soul inside because I could not understand why I felt such disgust. Weeks, then months had passed with this burden following me every waking moment. My thoughts began to shift.

I remembered a time, a few years earlier, when my mom and I were walking down the road, and I picked up a magazine from the ditch. Bare breasts covered most of the front page. I couldn't understand why females would pose naked. Disturbed but captivated, I stared intently at the pictures. My mom snatched it from my hands when she saw it and said, "paska!" She rarely swore, but when she was very upset, she would use the word "shit." She tossed it far into the bushes, and I tried to erase the disturbing images from my mind. When I'm a woman, my clothes would only come off for my husband, I thought.

After Ronnie, I started to see that I was now destined to become one of those women in the magazines. That's what men wanted and expected. Magazines were invented for them, and I was marked for life. I had been coerced into the realm of sexuality that I was definitely not ready for; my body was for the enjoyment of a male. No longer fit to be wife material, I was tarnished, un-pure, then I received an added stab in the heart; our house sold and we were to move into the city.

My parents were giving up my future home. I was livid and felt betrayed by everyone, even Jesus. Mom had mentioned something about looking for a home in the city previously, but I thought it might be a long-term goal. I assumed if she was serious, it would not happen until after I completed high school. I was in the prime of my childhood years. My freedom, and the very place where I still had some solace left, would be gone. I could not understand why my life turned upside down. Darkness was in my future, and I fell into a lonely hole of depression.

Chapter 13

## INNER RAGE

I was losing my classmates, my freedom to explore, and everything that I loved. Soon I would be in the city, in a different house and school. *I may as well be in prison.* I begged my mom for a little compassion to allow me to finish grade eight with my friends, but she had no power. The moving date was set, and in the fall, my world would forever change. My dad needed an easier lifestyle as he aged. The old guy now had to drive to the mailbox because he was breathless halfway through the walk. Our house sat on a hill which had a steep incline at the very top, and he feared he might not make it back to the door. His body started slowing down in his fifties, and he rested a lot more than usual. Years of hard work was catching up to him. Dad needed city life convenience, and Mom did not want to be stranded in the country without him. All I understood was that I was losing my freedom and horses and being thrown into jail without committing a crime.

Accepting the loss of everything I loved, was something I was not prepared to do. I wished for the day when Mom would tell me that it was not true, but that never happened. Death seemed like a good option, but I still believed I'd go straight to hell if I committed suicide. I had to weigh the options; suffer alone with my hidden turmoil or kill myself and be thrown into a flaming inferno. *What could I do?* My soul carried a heavy burden, and no one could help. I needed release. There was no talking to my parents, who had already made the decision without considering me.

In my bedroom, I locked the door and rummaged through my nightstand. I found a pocketknife and thought about plunging it deep into my chest. *Hell might not be so bad.* The blade was about three inches long, and I tested its sharpness with my finger. It was rather dull but would work. I slowly pushed it against my skin and sliced a couple of good gashes into my hand by my wrist. My delicate skin split like paper, and the pain oozed out with the blood trickling down my thumb, seeping into my brown bedroom carpet. I sat on my bed with tears of relief and rehearsed a few believable stories, to ward off any suspicions about the band-aides. For a moment, the turmoil was gone, and I knew I could turn to self-harm in the future if I needed release.

Every day after school, when the bus took me home, I kicked down the realtor sign at the start of our long driveway. I didn't want to look at the word, “SOLD,” and I’d be happy if the company never sold another house again - they ruined lives. I left graffiti with my markers under the rug in my play area, and hacked away at a beam under the stairs with a knife, leaving a mess of splintered wood. The thought of a new family taking over my house angered me. The new owners overlooked the minor vandalism, as it didn’t sway their final decision to purchase our home, and soon it was theirs.

The clock *ticked*, and I tried to enjoy the last of my life in the country, although this proved to be challenging. I couldn’t say goodbye… I didn’t know how to. My friends had a going-away party and wished me well in my new adventure. I felt the love of my classmates one last time before facing my fate. The day was bitter-sweet. The well-wishes were thoughtful, but I belonged in my country school with my friends. There should be no going-away party at all. I was touched by the love, but my heart stung knowing doomsday was nearby. As the days came and went, my rage grew fierce, and with nowhere to go, it finally reached the boiling point. My sixty-pound body was fuelled with desperation and vengeance. I needed to act out, to free myself of my pain, then I spotted our Buster sleeping on my bed. He was our little dog and I lashed out at the innocent creature by trying to end his life.

I pounced on top of him with a comforter to suffocate the helpless animal. He thrashed for his life, and nearing the end, his bowels were no longer in his control; he defecated on the blanket. My piercing eyes spotted the feces, and I became a deranged beast preying on the helpless. My skin turned red, and the stench of death filled the air. My mission: kill! His passing would signify the release of ugly shame within me. I didn't know how else to escape. His nose occasionally found a breath beyond the thick blanket, but I would catch him and tighten up the sack I'd made from the blanket. He would try to flee, but I was one step ahead of him. My teeth clenched together like the jaws of a pit bull, my body trembled, and I heard rapid tapping coming from somewhere. My heart pounded my chest wall with such force, I thought it would burst open. I didn't know this much fury could exist. I had exhausted myself, and Buster would live another day. My soul was cold. Dead.

Adults hadn't seemed to notice the rage in me. If Buster had died, maybe then they'd be forced to intervene. I was skilled at building walls of protection and secrecy. This would be the path to my addiction, later in life. I carried the shame of Ronnie, too terrified to tell anyone and cause a fuss. I could never tell anyone about Dad's brutalities because I must've done something bad to deserve his treatment. Fathers are not supposed to inflict fear on their children or pets, but he did, and I couldn't understand why. My cat would scurry away when he heard Dad's footsteps coming, in fear of a kick to the gut. From an early age, I must have known somewhere in my mind that this was dysfunctional. If anyone knew about my rage towards my dog, I'd be locked up. Bad things would happen to my entire family. These ugly truths must be hidden.

Guilt and shame would again fill my heart because of the terror I had inflicted on Buster. I loved him, and he trusted me up until that point, now he feared me; I feared myself more. *I am a psychopath.* Something abnormal dwelled in me, and I absolutely hated myself.

Moving day came, and we arrived at our city home, a brown brick bungalow with a tiny front and back yard. Everything about the house was small compared to where we used to live in the country. The main level had two bedrooms. Jari moved in with us while he studied nursing, and he took the big bedroom in the basement that we fought over, so my dad turned the storage area into a fourth bedroom for me. It was bigger than the closet-sized room upstairs, so I liked it. Jari kept busy with school and didn't bother me much. The house was in a decent residential neighborhood with a cemetery just minutes away, where I could roam around the paths and headstones. The far end felt like the country. Overgrown bush, grass, and the scent of food brought wildlife like deer and black bears to the area. There was a hidden baseball field nearby and a walking path following the river up to a bridge. On one side were backyards of houses, but most of the homes had shrubbery providing some privacy from people enjoying the river walk.

No matter which window I looked out of in our new place, a house blocked my view. I didn't see fields, the barn or horses. I saw brick houses, pavement, small trimmed shrubs, and people. Sometimes the couple next door would be outside, sitting in their tiny yard or raking up fallen leaves from their perfect lawn. The crowding gave me claustrophobia; there was no privacy. I spent a lot of time indoors, hiding in the basement. I didn't want to face the neighbors intruding on my space and seeing every move I made. Traffic could usually be heard from a busy street nearby, and the city bus route traveled just one street away from my house. The sounds of sirens were also a common occurrence - silence was rare. People casually strolled right in front of the house with their dogs daily, and apparently, this was normal. At home, when I saw a car or a passerby, I'd run to the window with binoculars; it would be the neighbors or Johanna coming over. Gawking at people with binoculars was frowned upon by city folks. The city had all kinds of rules and restrictions that the country never had.

My parents told me about a public school only three blocks away. I was somehow supposed to be excited about being forced to go to a stupid school in the stupid city. I didn't know anyone there, so I refused to go. All I wanted to do was move back home and join my classmates, but that was not an option. I chose another school, out of my zone, where my nephews attended. I thought I might see a familiar face, even though their class was at the junior end of the school. I fought hard to have a choice, to have a vote in this matter, as my choices prior to this had been stripped away. Reluctantly, my parents agreed. Part of their hesitancy was because the school was out of my district, so bussing was not available. I would have to walk when Dad could not drive me; although, he had more free days, being recently retired.

When Dad was busy, I walked. Mom would have to come with me because the town was not safe. I could walk for days in the country, but a mile or so in the city is different. As we passed pedestrians on the sidewalk, I always gave them the once over, just in case. If an attack were to occur, this time I would be ready to fight them off, at least that's what I'd say to myself. In reality I'd yank my mom's arm and scream, "Juokse! Juokse!"

City kids differed from country kids. Many smoked, used profanity, and some were bullies - this life wasn't for me. I missed Johanna, Pam and everything about Kam. We all had each others' backs and "damn" was a swear word that we sometimes dared to say when we were sassy. I felt alone and forgotten. There was one friend in the world who always comforted me, my cuddly cat Puss in Boots, but he was lost in Kam.

Chapter 14

## PUSS IN BOOTS

The horses and Johanna still lived in Kam, and so did Puss. On moving day, the U-Haul truck was loaded, and it brought our belongings to the city, but we left Puss behind. My dad had no intention of bringing him along with us. I was crushed, and I despised the man that I called Isä. His cruelty not only affected me, but Puss was alone, scared, and dumped. Puss would wonder why I left him. Dad was the only way to Kam, and if anyone could change his mind, it would be Mom. Four agonizing weeks passed and Mom finally convinced him to get the cat. She begged on my behalf, and I think he didn't want to hear her nagging anymore, so he agreed.

With Dad behind the wheel, and me in the passenger seat, the truck rumbled down the familiar highway we'd traveled for years. I was going to find my cat, no matter what! I was hopeful, but anxiety filled me at the possibility that we would not be reunited. I focused on the twists and turns of the road, remembering being snuggled on my mom's lap after the town business was done; it was the best place to be. My cheek snuggled into her fur collar, secured by her arms. Her voice would softly hum a hymn, and her fingertips lightly scratched my back to let me know she was there. I wished Mom was with us now, and I was sitting on her lap, but I wasn't a little girl anymore.

We turned onto Hill Road and drove up the driveway of our old home. Dad told me the wolves had probably gotten to the cat – I'm sure he was hoping so. I did not look at the house or make eye contact with the new owners. *Dad can chat with them and explain why he left Puss there. This house was no longer mine, and I was there for one reason only; to rescue Puss.* I called for him and set out a can of tuna I'd brought with me, to lure him to the food. Despite the time he'd been alone, I still had hope for Puss' survival. With every passing minute gone by without Puss, my heart thumped an extra beat. My eyes were laser focused as I scanned the empty field, the riverbank, and random woodpiles, looking for any sign of movement. I was anxious and hoped Dad didn't want to leave yet. He had zero patience, and when he decided it was time to go, we would; with or without Puss. *I may never see my cuddly companion again.*

I said a silent prayer, *God, please tell Puss to come out from wherever he is hiding. I am here to rescue him.* Not long after, the sound of faint meowing came from the long grass. The grass swayed from side to side, as if an invisible force were coming through, and then the majestic white and black spotted fur of Puss appeared on the driveway. I stood up from the bridge, and my heart swelled with joy! I wanted to run to him, but I let him walk towards me, then I scooped him up and cradled him in my arms, kissing his battered face.

Majestic isn't a word others would use to describe Puss. He was flea-ridden, dirty and hid from everyone besides me or Mom, but beauty is in the beholder's eye and to me, despite his shriveled-up body and swollen face, he was magnificent. His cheek was scratched and swollen; he'd been fighting for his life in the wild, but now he'd be safe.

The ride home in the noisy truck terrified Puss, and he moaned and groaned the entire half-hour drive to town. I tried to calm him and held him close to me, leaning towards the door, to keep him as far away as possible from my dad. "It's ok, Puss, you're safe now," I whispered to him. "You'll be okay." I kept Puss's face nestled into my jacket while I gazed at the empty highway. My heart had a piece of comfort now, and with the love of my cat, it made letting go of my former life a little easier - we would get through this together.

Dad and I didn't talk on the way back to town. Instead, I zoned into thoughts about the rescue mission and memories of my prior life and horses. Johanna's family welcomed me to enjoy country freedom with them, but it hurt too much. I tried, but it only reminded me that Kam was no longer my home, and strangers lived in my house. I had to accept my dismal future without horses and the confinement of city living; depression struck. I kept my eyes glued to the treetops from the side window so Dad wouldn't see my tears. Joyful memories and pain all rolled into one streamed down my cheeks. My mind wandered to the dense evergreens at the top of the sliding hill and the "bases" my nieces, nephews, and I made while playing war.

Our long driveway had a small bridge over a stream, leading to the pond that occasionally needed repairs, and we had to walk over the bridge carrying groceries; as the structure would collapse with the weight of a vehicle. Close to the pond was the clearest, calmest water I'd ever seen. When I knelt next to the watering hole, and the ripples disappeared, my reflection stared back at me. As a child, it was amazing to see yourself in a puddle of water, but this water was no puddle; this was a natural spring. I could see my sun freckles, my slightly crooked front tooth, and there was no hiding the two wild cowlicks on either side of my forehead that I could never tame. The floor of the spring was home to rocks, algae, and frogs. Sometimes when I put my lips to the surface of the water, a frog would emerge from his hiding spot and glide through the icy cold water. Life flourished in this peaceful, natural place, and I never disturbed this sanctuary. Natural spring water never came out of our taps in the city; that water was infused with chlorine, and who knows what, which made it taste awful - I hated it.

I was furious at my parents about the move and thoughts of revenge began to overtake my brain. I lost my home and horses because of them, and they deserved my rage. Although, the truth for my pain was more about Ronnie, and my parents had no fault in that. The move to the city was the perfect way to deflect my anger. No one can know the real root of my behaviour and depression.

When we finally arrived in Thunder Bay, I introduced Puss to his new home, which was my bedroom. We would stay in the basement most of the time. I had his food dish downstairs and his litter box in the bathroom. I gave him a sponge bath and inspected the gash on his face, which likely came from another cat. There was no chance of a vet visit, when a bullet was cheaper, so I did the best I could to heal it. Puss did not like the band-aide I applied, so I just tried to keep it clean. One day after school, I came home to an image that would forever be etched in my mind.

It was 3:15 pm, and the last bell of the day chimed. I changed my shoes and raced out the door to see my mom waving at me from across the street. At thirteen years old, I didn't want her picking me up from my classroom, but I needed her there. We had a twenty-minute walk, and we chatted about my siblings and the gorgeous autumn day. I wanted to get home and put on my shorts one more time.

The truck sat in the driveway, so I knew Dad was home. The lawn was mowed. No one was outside, and there was nothing unusual about that day. I walked ahead of Mom along the side of the house and turned the corner to walk up the four cement steps to the door, as I'd been doing for a few weeks now - Puss was there. He lay on the top stair with blood oozing from his head, dripping from stair to stair, a deep hole in the side of his head. My knees buckled beneath me, and I reached for the handrail on the stairs. I sat on the stairs stroking Puss's body as tears escaped my eyes. My heart splintered into a million pieces just as it had begun to mend. My Puss in Boots was gone. I thought I had brought him home safe but instead, I brought him into the clutches of a madman. I was destroyed by Dad's cruelty.

Mom glanced at Puss, and slowly shook her head while covering her face with both hands. She tiptoed past Puss and me, into the house. I could hear her yelling at my dad, but my sobs muffled her words. My stomach tightened into a knot. I didn't know how I would go on without Puss by my side. He would lay close to my face during the nights when I tried to cry the shame away, and now, he was gone. I pet Puss's still warm body for the last time, opened the door, and saw my dad's shotgun leaning against the wall in the porch. I ran down to my room, locked myself in, and cried uncontrollably. How can one man be so cruel?

We were country folk, and shooting a sick animal was not uncommon, but this kill was evil. Puss had a scratch; he was not sick. I knew Dad must've heard Puss meowing for something, and that triggered him into kill-mode. He didn't give any thought to his family or city bylaws. I had no warning, no chance for goodbyes, no chance to plead for his life. I rescued Puss from the wilderness just a few days ago, and before leaving for school in the morning, I kissed him, then came home to a crime scene. Dad didn't utter a word to me. What could he say?

The sun would still rise each day, and I would face my dad daily. I wanted to injure him, make him feel the pain he caused Puss and me. The horrific incident could not be processed by my brain. I was forced to create an altered reality to protect my well-being. My mind conjured up a scenario about the scratches on Puss's face, telling me that the injury on his face was deadly, he would never have healed, and he was on his death bed. This is a story that I could almost wrap my mind around; this was a little piece of reasoning for his heinous actions. How else would I be able to call him Isä? I would never forgive him and gave up on trying to figure out my father's insanity. I was done with him.

Chapter 15

## RUM AND COKE

Without Puss by my side, grade eight was long and depressing. My heart ached for him every day, and the shock of how he died was too painful to accept. Puss was gone, my former classmates were gone, and I hated being the new kid, trying to fit in where I absolutely did not belong. I came into my new school feeling broken, bitter and depressed. No one knew the secrets of my life, the transition was traumatic, but eventually, I made a few buddies and even had a date for the graduation ceremony. I survived my final year of public school by fantasizing about high school, which gave me a glimmer of hope for the future.

After grade eight graduation, I cut my hair, dyed it bleach blonde, and started crimping it; I needed to put the year behind me, and become someone else - anyone but Anita. High school was approaching, and new adventures were to come. Johanna was excited and eager to explore the city in my area. School was out, summer was in. We reconnected and wanted adventure again, but the rebellious kind. I was thirsty for retaliation against my parents, God, the world, to everyone for causing me pain. My parents would pay for forcing me into the confinement of the city, and I would do all the things they hated. This was the beginning of my descent.

Johanna spent time at my house, and we traveled by foot to parks, beaches and hung out at the mall buying fantastic outfits. At times, we'd leave the change room slightly bigger than when we went in. I was surprised the staff never caught on, but we did look young and innocent. Our hormones went wild, and we stalked the cute boys. Before hitting high school, we both had boyfriends and our first taste of alcohol.

I was thirteen when our neighbor's daughter got married. The reception was held at a small community hall. I'd been to church weddings before but never to the after-party. Johanna and her family were also there. While the adults mingled, they expected us to clear the tables. The room was dark. A few guests sat at the tables, but most were on the dance floor. After dinner, the room was dimmed, and the disco ball lights began flashing; the party was on. This was the first time for both Johanna and me, to be in an environment of music and alcohol.

While the adults socialized, Johanna and I retrieved a metal cart from the kitchen and loaded it with dirty dishes. Several glasses still had wine or champagne in them. Together, we decided to have a taste. My mom always preached about not wasting; I was taking her advice, but of course, she never would've approved me of drinking wine. She would've thrown it directly down the toilet. I picked up half a glass of pale golden champagne and almost drowned myself. I had to act quickly before being spotted by an adult. The aroma was pleasant; it tasted like bubbly sweet juice. My tongue had a happy tingle, and the bubbles popped in my mouth as the alcohol disappeared down my throat, no one saw a thing. "That was sweet! I didn't know wine tasted like that!" I smacked my hand on my mouth to stop a bout of upcoming outrageous laughter. Johanna looked away from me and did the same. We didn't want to draw attention to us with all the alcohol we still planned to drink. I couldn't believe what I'd just done.

"We are so bad, Un-Bun! We better not get caught, or our parents will kill us!"

She was right; we felt like we were bad asses and would have been banned from seeing each other forever, if caught. We loaded up the cart and combined leftovers of wine, champagne, and beer - our own cocktail. We tried to quietly creep down the dim hallway with the cart back to the kitchen so that we could chug back the glasses of mixed booze. After a few trips with the cart, the tables were cleared, and our tummies were full. Everything seemed normal at first, and then it hit us. Our heads spun, like when we had twirled around in circles a hundred times before trying to walk. Our words got mumbled, and we giggled at our goofiness. Johanna and I experienced an act of adulthood together.

I floated far from all the agony that lived inside me, and for the first time, my pain was gone. I found the answer to life, but how would I ever get alcohol again at age thirteen? I danced the night away and wound up in the arms of a fellow in his thirties, who passionately kissed me. I allowed him to have his way; it was what I knew. My family members spotted us on the crowded dance floor and yanked him aside. The prominent lawyer was busted. *Sucker*.

The days of immortality, and the terrible teen years were upon me. I became a wild child without a thought about safety or my future. Johanna and I roamed the city day and night, waving at the fast cars as they cruised the streets on Saturday nights, blasting AC/DC's Highway to Hell. The 80s were the good old days where doors stayed unlocked, safety could be found with block parents, and 10 o'clock curfews for minors were enforced; still, danger existed in the world.

The summer after the wedding, I had turned fourteen. Johanna and I had arranged a sleepover at my house but sleeping was not what we had in mind. Her mom dropped her off, and when my parents were fast asleep, we planned to sneak out and party all night. We walked up to Red River Road, which was the main drag for cruise night, and we were sure a car full of cute boys would let us know where the house parties were. As we strolled down the street, they'd whistle out of their car windows, and we would giggle and wave, loving the attention.

Later in the evening, a middle-aged man stopped and asked if we wanted a ride. Of course we did; he had a fancy red sports car and was able to buy alcohol. He could become our booze dealer. He wasn't our parent, so I'm sure he wouldn't have an issue supplying us with a few drinks, even though we were underage. We knew we must take advantage of this amazing opportunity and did not hesitate to hop into the stranger's ride. He drove us around the town from the north end to the south end. He drove by all the parking spots where kids hung out, blasting their tunes from the trunk of their souped-up cars. The stranger's ride was not a decked-out car with flames or stripes. It was stylish, clean, and new. We were having a blast, being all cool, driving around in his expensive car. We stopped at a park overlooking the bright lights of the city. The man asked if we wanted to go to his place for a drink. The words we'd been longing to hear finally graced our ears.

He lived in a classy area with old character homes, shutters framed the windows, and a new deck wrapped halfway around the residence. He seemed like a responsible working man, like an average white dude. He was not a large man, rather small and wimpy looking, casually dressed in a button-up shirt.

I had no inkling of danger and felt good about being with Johanna because the two of us could put up a mean fight if he did try anything funny. Johanna and I had each other as we followed the scrawny little man downstairs. The den had dark brown shag carpeting, a large floor model TV, and a grey, puffy couch that leaned against one wall, with striped wallpaper behind it. The air had a touch of deadness to it. He shut the door behind us. In the room's corner was a liquor cabinet filled with a variety of liquid gold.

"What would you like to drink?" he asked as he walked towards the liquor.

"Champagne?" I said, awkwardly. I didn't know much about naming alcoholic beverages, but I knew about champagne.

"I'm all out," he said as he opened the liquor cabinet. "But I think you might like this." He gathered some glasses from the cabinet while Johanna and I whispered about hitting the booze jackpot.

I anticipated the carefree experience I'd had before with champagne, floating about, without a care in the world. Alcohol brought me to happiness, and I needed that escape again; to live in a silly world, if even for a moment. Soon I would experience the glorious get-away again. He prepared three glasses of rum and coke, then put them in our waiting hands. The fancy glass touched my lips, and I immediately noticed the smell of sweet liquorice; this was not regular coke. I did not hesitate and took a big gulp. It warmed my mouth with a loving combination of sugar, vanilla and a touch of spice.

"What do you think, Johanna?" I asked.

"It's freakin' awesome!" she said. The man held up his glass, and we all cheered to us; me, my bestie, and our new connection to booze - the scrawny little man.

I liked coke, but now it tasted even better. "This is the best invention ever!" I said, beaming with delight. We made ourselves comfortable on the couch, giggling about drinking rum and coke in the man cave. I finished my drink and rather quickly, the room seemed to be a million miles away. My vision began to blur, and I clutched the side of the couch, as my strength was dissipating quickly. I thought I might flop onto the floor at any minute. Why was this happening? Drinking was supposed to be fun, it made me giddy and wobble, but this feeling was something unfamiliar. I glanced at Johanna and wondered if we would get out of there to party with boys, as we had planned. We thought we were wise and aware of any potential attack, because we were intelligent teenagers who knew *everything* about the world. This man couldn't take the two of us down easily, so he had another plan - one we never suspected. The booze pit stop may be our last stop, ever. We were at his mercy.

My eyelids are heavy. I am fighting to keep them open. The room is spinning around me, and I'm starting to feel limp like I'm being phased out. I see the man in front of me through a small slit between my lashes. He is a silhouette - no features. He is moving the coffee table. *Why?* My tumbler glass is empty with a few ice cubes on the bottom. It slips out of my fingers onto the shag carpet. I ask Johanna, “Do you feel dizzz-eee?” That is my last memory. I enter a time warp where I no longer exist, and my body is not my own. Slowly I begin to arouse to a muffled male voice, but I can’t understand what he is saying. I am lying on a sofa-bed with my clothes tousled on my body. Johanna is sitting next to me, putting her shoes on. He is the scrawny little man with the sports car. “What happened? What time is it?” I ask. I don’t know if we’ve been there for ten minutes or ten hours.

“Time for you to leave,” he replies. Now he seems rude, impatient. Maybe his wife is about to come home, or he wants us out while we’re still alive. He grabs our purses and says, “get moving.” He shoves us out the door into the darkness.

The streetlights are glowing. It is still night as we head south towards my house. No parties for us that night. We are groggy and tired. Neither one of us could explain what occurred in the man cave, yet we knew – a huge gap of time disappeared. Whatever secret potion he gave us emptied our minds; the hours were blank. This would be our unspoken secret, too frightening to discuss. Weeks later, odd flashbacks appear out of nowhere. I see his back and hear the *glug-glugs* of rum and coke being poured into our glasses, *his smug eyes,* while he hands us our drinks, and I feel scruffy chin whiskers on my thighs—a feeling of sickening violation. The lure of drinks was irresistible to us but, we did not expect to vanish.

There would be no justice; it was probably our fault anyway, as we willingly got into his car. Neither one of us wanted to expose this night. The thought of cops, rape kits, and people knowing, was far too much drama for us to deal with. I'd rather die than translate these words for my parents. I didn't want to be a courtroom spectacle, being referred to as the victim. People would peg me as weak and deserving of rape, because I chose to enter his house. I immediately took the blame, tucked it into my box of shame, and called it a day.

Chapter 16

## OBLIVION

The missing hours permanently changed the way I thought about myself. I decided that I would NEVER be a victim again. No one would ever take advantage of me again. If I sensed a losing battle, I'd give in and be submissive; this would be my delusion of giving permission. You can't be a victim if you never say "no". That was my new plan, as I was still worlds away from having the power to say no and mean it. The traumas altered my rational thinking, and this made sense to me. I'd been called lush, basket-case, psycho, and much worse, but being called a victim signified that I was weak and that, I felt, was the worst insult ever.

Thoughts of the man cave made me cringe. Who else was in the room? Was it recorded? I would never know. The creepy molester should be locked up, but fear and my foggy memory kept me from speaking out. There was only one way to deal with the disturbing flashbacks - alcohol-induced oblivion. But getting my hands on it would not be a simple task.

# Box of Shame

The strongest drink in my home was my parent's leftover coffee from the day before. I wasn't interested in a caffeine fix, I needed the good stuff, and my boyfriend Tony's house had plenty of vino. An Italian dinner table without wine was sacrilegious. Johanna and I met Tony and his friend in a park playground where teens often hung out. The sun had set, but I spotted his white T-shirt, light grey jeans, muscles, and adorable dimples from a distance.

"Cute boy alert!" I whisper to Johanna. "There's two of them."

"What should we say? They look older."

"I don't know Johanna, let's try to act mature, okay?"

Johanna unzipped her jacket as we walked straight towards the guys. Tony was dreamy. His hair was short but long enough to show his black curls. We had a connection from the first glance, and I thought about how to get his phone number without having to ask for it, because that would seem desperate. - I was, but I didn't want him to know. His friend had a girlfriend, so it was not Johanna's lucky night. We chatted in the park for a while, and Tony offered his number. I felt like the luckiest girl on earth.

The three of us became a trio, Tony, me, and Johanna. I had many family dinners at his house with his elderly parents and siblings. They accepted me as part of the family and let me drink homemade wine, or should I say, expected me to. Johanna often joined us. I didn't particularly like the bitter taste, but I loved how it made me pain-free. I paced myself at the table, trying to drink like everyone else. When Mr. Brunetti picked up the wine decanter to top up everyone's glass, I casually pushed mine towards him. I wanted seconds, thirds, while others were often satisfied with just one glass. Why have one, when you can have two or three or an entire bottle!

Mr. and Mrs. Brunetti raised their children to drink wine at the table, and when I was there, I would do the same. However, every glass of wine I had, covered up secrets they didn't know about, and I didn't want them to know. I was full of shame and humiliation from being victimized by an old pervert on the loose. They didn't know about my dad's outrageous behaviors and my constant state of anxiety and depression. The wine was my medicine to help with these pains.

Finally, high school began. I was a junior, and Tony was a senior, so that placed me in the popular category. I had the cute Italian boy who wore Drakkar Noir aftershave, which drove the girls wild. I felt alive again and happy. Johanna, Tony, and I often hung out together at school. Pam spent her spare time with her boyfriend getting serious about marriage. We all drank in high school, and sometimes Pam would join us, but she respected her parent's curfew. She wasn't on the same rebellious streak that I was on. When it was time to go, she just left. Although the hard-drinking lifestyle wasn't hers, she did not have one judgmental bone in her body.

Tony was by my side throughout grade nine, even though my dad forbade the relationship after he first saw me intoxicated on Tony's couch. Dad's attempts only pushed me deeper into the arms of Tony; however, our young love did not last. I was not a mature, confident teen capable of relationships. Our relationship started to fall apart by the time grade 10 rolled around. I was jealous, insecure, and had no self-worth. Tony started seeing other girls, and when I found out who had all his attention, the prank calls began. I'd call his new girlfriend and breathe heavily into the phone or scratch at the mouthpiece with my fingernails. She knew it was me, even though I did not say any words on the phone. After a dozen times, she threatened to call the cops, so I felt justified to scream, "Call the cops bitch, I dare you!" If she had any doubts about if I was the prank caller, I just erased them for her.

At midnight, the cops pulled into my driveway, with flashing red and blue lights, but no siren. My dad runs outside. *The bitch actually called the cops!* I peek out of my bedroom window from the basement and see Dad's legs from the knees down, talking to a man in blue. I panic, run out of my room, up the stairs, and fly out the door, attempting to keep the situation under control. “Everything is fine, it's under control, don’t worry!” The officer tells me about a complaint of harassment made against me and charges could be laid. I am steaming mad but play it cool. My dad is standing in the driveway with a look of confusion, trying to get answers. He’s wondering why the cops are there, and I’m glad the officer isn’t fluent in Finn. I quickly tell the officer that I would never call her again, and it was just a silly fight we had.

He is satisfied and says, “I hope I don’t have to come back, because I will lay harassment charges if I get another call about you.”

“Don’t worry; you won’t have to come back,” I promised him.

He nods at my dad before walking to his squad car and drives away. I look at my dad and blurt, "there was a problem with the phone, and I accidentally called the police; that's why he came." If the policeman used words like 'prank calls' or 'harassment,' my dad would've never picked up on why the officer was there. However, if he heard words like, 'drunk, drinking, or trouble,' he'd have a good idea about why the police showed up. Dad had no clue that I was in the basement obsessively pounding the number keys and breathing like a creeper on the phone. From his perspective, I was safe at home for one night sober, and that's all he really cared about.

Our young and immature teenage love ended. I lost the boy and felt as if I might die from heartbreak. I shed many tears at night, crying over my first love. Again, my pocketknife helped to ease the pain and a few notches were added to my wrist. Johanna tried to console me, and we became Tony haters. The break-up *must* be all his fault. He's a fool to leave an insane jealous drunk who could snap at any minute. *He doesn't know what he's lost. He'll live to regret it!* I tried to convince myself of lies like this, because facing the truth of my mental health issues and addictions was too painful. Living a lie was much easier.

"Un-Bun, you're better off without him. You'll find someone better." Johanna helped me get through my first heartbreak.

"Screw that… no more guys for me! I'm staying single forever!" Forever was short-lived. Within a week or so, I'd be hooked up with someone again because I didn't know who I was or how to be alone, and a boyfriend was my way to alcohol.

The bottle would be my comfort. I drank to oblivion on weekends and usually made it home by 5 a.m., before my parents woke up. The drinking freed me and armed me with false confidence. Without my liquid courage, I was the wallflower, silent and incapable of natural conversation. After a few drinks, I'd bust out of my shell, jabbering, and becoming the life of the party. It all was dependant on how much I drank.

One time, after a night on the town, I hitched a ride with my friend Shane and his buddy. Neither of the boys knew where I lived, and apparently, I didn't either. The ride started from one end of town and zig zagged in every direction. The driver needed more information other than Thunder Bay. "What is the name of the street you live on?"

I slurred saying, "Itza bron hozzz in da graaaave yaaaard."

My mouth could not vocalize coherent speech, only slurring and babble came out. The driver was losing patience with my mixed-up directions. We stopped at several brown houses by the cemetery in my neighborhood, but none were mine. At some point during the drive, I blacked out. Had it not been for Shane, who knows where I would have ended up?

"I'm just gonna dump her on the fucken street!" The chauffeur is livid and can't handle my nonsense anymore.

"No, we can't leave her on the street; look at her," Shane said. "I'll try to get it out of her."

Shane convinced him to pull over and get me out of the car for some fresh night air. They were both sick of the aimless travel. The cool breeze perked me up enough to tell him where I lived. With no cell phones or Google maps to rely on, finding addresses were challenging, especially when drunk. At about 4:15 a.m., Shane walked me to my back door, and then they left.

Late in the afternoon the next day, I woke up safe in my waterbed. I had the odd flash of the night before, but most of it was blank. I remembered sitting in the back seat of a car but couldn't recall being dropped off at home. I called Shane to help fill in the blanks. He explained the frustrating driving about, as he had never been to my house before. His friend got so erratic; he was going to dump me in the cemetery.

"Shit, man, I don't remember any of that," I said. I felt terrible but thankful that he was there. "So, you walked me to my room?" I continued.

"No, I checked the door. It was open, so I figured as long as you got inside, you'd be fine."

"Really? I don't know how I got down the steep stairs without killing myself. That's so strange." I tried to remember getting to my room.

I wondered if my dad helped me down the stairs or if I slid down quietly enough not to wake my parents. Dad never peeped a word about the night, and I wasn't going to ask. Maybe due to Mom's daily prayers, an angel carried me safely to my bed. I wouldn't be surprised.

After experiencing blackouts, it appeared obvious to others that my drinking was out of control. I thought they were amateurs, and I was not ready to hear about giving up the alcohol. When I sensed others giving me the look of, "Hey, I think you've had enough," I immediately found ways of hiding it. I adjusted my drinking and behavior according to who was around me. I'd have to live separate lives, and because I was an addict and manipulator, I knew how to play the game. However, I still could not control how the night would end, after promising myself that it would be a fun night. No matter how good-intentioned I was, something bad usually happened. After one drunken night, recovery became an option, but it wasn't exactly my choice.

I'd been hanging out often at a party house and punched out a bedroom window – a display of "look at me, I'm tough." Short girls always seem to have something to prove, and I tried to build an image of 'short but tough', because I was just over five feet tall. If I lashed out violently, every now and then, it would keep me safe from being victimized. People were freaking out once they noticed the blood. "Why did she punch out the window?" I heard from the other room. "It was just an accident, people!" I hollered at no one in particular, while a friend handed me a towel to stop the bleeding.

I can't recall how I got to the hospital, but there I was, laying on a hospital bed, a drunken mess with a couple of my siblings close by. I was ashamed of what I had become, but more ashamed that they were witnessing me in this condition. The only question I remember asking is, “Is Mom here?” I had never faced her drunk and never wanted to. I’d be too ashamed of causing her pain. Thankfully, she was not there. My siblings knew that my self-induced condition would break her heart. We did everything we could to protect her from emotional pain, only telling her what was necessary.

I can overhear a few words between the nurse and my family. “Possible alcohol poisoning… future”. I was annoyed that they would not talk to me about this, but I was in no condition to communicate anyway. I left with four stitches in my hand, after a few small shards of glass were removed. What started as a revenge plot against my parents now became like a wildfire, out of my control. My friends and siblings worried, but most of all my plan was destroying me. I couldn’t stop my destructive mode.

My parents had dealt with enough of my late-night drinking episodes. I would have to work harder to hide my drinking from them. I didn’t want to continue to worry them, but my main concern was the fear that I may be separated from alcohol. When the nurses recommended rehab, it seemed unfair that they made a judgment about me, assuming I had a problem - they didn’t know me.

Drinking was the solution to life, and it helped me to survive. Rehab would take it away, and I would die.

Maybe things were getting a little out of hand, but I just had to stay away from windows while drinking. I could not imagine sober living; no one did that. My toxic relationship with alcohol would have to be a secret from my family. I brought shame to them and was a terrible role model to the youngest ones in the family. I was a failure. I doubted I'd even see the age of 25, and I didn't care. The long-lost dreams of a family, nursing, and becoming an artist were fading into a life meant for someone else. I had drinking to do.

My sister arranged a therapy appointment for kids at risk of addiction after my ER visit. It's funny that they thought I was *at risk;* I was already deep into the roots of my obsession. I couldn't talk my way out of this, so I agreed to one session. It was a better choice than rehab. I sat in the waiting area, rapidly bouncing my knee, and sliding my sweaty hands up and down my thighs. I had no desire to talk to Jody; therapy is for the weak.

I felt the eyes of a waiting room mom glance at me every so often as she pretended to read a magazine. I was nervous, but I looked presentable, like a typical 80s teen: skin-tight jeans, belly top, large hoop earrings, and my favorite "pretty in pink" lipstick. My hair was perfectly curled, with enough hairspray to withstand a hurricane, and my Harley Davidson purse held the essentials such as, makeup, smokes, and some change. Her staring made me feel like judgment was upon me. *I need a drink.* I was not looking forward to this appointment. I got up and headed for the door.

I looked at the secretary and said, "I'll be back in a minute, just going out for a smoke."

When I came back in, she escorted me to the therapist's office at the end of the hall. A casually dressed young man with long sleek hair and round spectacles sat in his oversized leather chair behind his desk. *Jody is a male? Perfect, this is going to be a huge waste of time!* There were papers and a few psychology books stacked on the side, along with a photo of him and his pretty blonde girlfriend. A cactus stood in the corner near the window; the whole setup was made to feel welcoming, but my anxiety didn't care.

He rose when I entered and reached out for a handshake. "Hi, my name's Jody, have a seat." A friendly guy, but still a man. He was going to try to make sense of the tangled mess inside my head.

Strike one: I came by force. Strike two: he's a male. I would never share my life details with anyone, especially him. I tried to cooperate and gave him enough answers to appease him. I began to loosen up and didn't mind the superficial chatting. He let me run the show, and I talked about all the wonderful parts of my life before the drinking started.

Then the tough questions came, "How old were you when you first started drinking? How are things at home?" He promised that even though I was only 15 years old, everything discussed had to be confidential, so no one except for he and I, would know about this conversation.

Maybe he had some magic words that would change my life. If I could fit into society, maintain a job, wake in the morning after a night of drinking, and not have regrets, what a great life that would be! *I should give this guy a chance, maybe I should tell him more about my past.* If we shared some common ground and trust, maybe there was hope for me, but first I needed to know more about him. He gave me some mumbo jumbo talk about how therapy works, but it was almost as if he was reading a textbook. He was nice enough, qualified, and well versed in the fancy lingo; I'm sure he'd dealt with addiction and crazy people before. But what I really needed was an alcoholic-to-alcoholic connection. Had he experienced alcoholism? Did he ever suffer?

“We are here to talk about you, not me,” was his response when I asked a personal question. My lips pursed together as the words, *Well, screw this! If you haven’t experienced this, you can’t possibly help me,* were at the tip of my tongue. This was going nowhere, and I shut down immediately. The brief flicker of hope I had was gone.

Chapter 17

# LOST

Some people prefer to forget about high school. It's an awkward time for many. Despite the heartaches and loss I endured, some good times were had. Dances, sports, and amazing teachers were some highlights. My drinking career was in full swing, and I experienced many drunken blackouts. It seemed odd to be told stories about an entire night where my mind was highjacked by alcohol, but my body was still active. When I heard the stories, sometimes I could only laugh and shake my head at the craziness.

At one backyard party, I climbed up onto a picnic table, stretched out my arms, and yelled, "TIIIMBEEER," as I dropped myself back off the table. A crowd of party goers caught me before I crashed onto the lawn. I can't recall what my mindset was at the time. It was a stunt for attention, I assume. Did I think I was Superwoman? After being caught crawling onto the table again, a couple of friends carried me inside because they didn't want to be my safety mat. Luckily, I didn't break my neck. Hidden blessings.

Other times, the day-after stories were disturbing. Too troublesome to be about me, too shameful to admit. One night, I recall arriving at a nice brick house with a fully furnished basement full of kids, drinking and smoking. Many of them went to my high school, while some came from other schools. My state of drunkenness reached its peak, and into the blackout, I descended. I became the life of the party and the main dish on a buffet table, unconscious and naked. It was a help-yourself kind of party, and some guys did.

These after party tales would have been sobering for anyone, but they only drove me deeper into my obsession. I didn't want to dig further into memory to bring up the scenario. I'd rather keep it forgotten. Even though a witness told me, I hoped that maybe it hadn't happened since I couldn't recall, but it seems to ring true in a sense. My value equaled garbage. My "life's calling" was to be useful to men, but only in the flesh. I was living my destiny, straight into the ditch I would be thrown once I was used up. Only liquor could hide my ugliness, and it helped me to forget. I didn't know how to live without it. Every day my heart would beat to a perfect rhythm, and the exchange of oxygen and $CO_2$ in my lungs continued. My body existed, but my essence was hiding behind a fake persona. This is not what social drinking looks like. I'd lost all restraint but admitting this was still years away.

With my compulsive behaviors on the forefront, drinking masked my misery and helped me enjoy high school. Whenever my shameful past began to surface, alcohol made it disappear. My friends and I got excited about football games even though I wasn't especially a football fan, but the exhilaration of the crowd pumped me up. The sound of the bass shook the stands as the green and white Colts charged the field. I wasn't the only one sneaking in a micky for the game.

School became an outlet away from home. Dad's behaviors mellowed out now that he was in his mid-sixties, and daily life no longer involved the usual chores of country living. But every now and then, he'd still have enough spunk in him to scream like a lunatic around the house. My siblings also visited home often, and I did not feel comfortable with them questioning my life. I had nothing good to say, no plans of becoming a teacher, nurse, or social worker, like them. My life goal was to find alcohol, and that took up my time and energy. We did not have common interests or goals, so I avoided home in fear of their disapproval.

I was old enough to distance myself from home, and I didn't miss school often, but I did miss class regularly. Johanna, sometimes Pam and I, would skip class and walk down to the waterfront for the best fries and gravy at Birds restaurant. It was always worth the absent check on my report card, but my parents didn't hassle me much about skipping class anyway. Communicating in English was difficult for them, so I did most of the translating. I dared teachers to call my mom when I got out of line. "Hello, this is Mr. Gainer calling about your daughter's continued absence from math class." I would translate this as, "He's just phoning to tell you how great I'm doing in class Mom, don't worry, it's all good!" Johanna was a little jealous. Her parents spoke English fluently, so she had to be creative when we missed class. Eventually, my parents grew suspicious and got my sisters involved. They explained the real meaning of the phone calls home—poor Mom and Dad.

My sister, Marja, was not impressed with me skipping class. She took her education seriously and encouraged us younger siblings to do the same. Her eyes were set on the future. Alcoholism was not a part of her story because she had plans of helping others as a nurse. She wanted independence and security, something none of us had in our household, and not long after graduation she moved to Toronto, Ontario, to work at the Wellesley Hospital. She was a beautiful person and made her mark in the world by choosing a career over a man. A domesticated housewife/mom would never be her role, but she did long for love.

The need for connection and romance had struck, and she chose a grumpy old man as a husband. I could not understand why she chose him. She visited home often, and sometimes we visited her in Toronto. She lived in the penthouse of a condominium, with the old man. He was gentle with me, but not to Marja. I loved my visits with Marja. She spoiled me and cooked fancy meals I'd never seen before. When her husband appeared, the air shifted, Marja's chatter trailed off, and her soft, lovely face transformed to stone. He bossed her around the minute he entered the room. People didn't know what was happening inside the walls of their marriage, but some eyebrows were raised - perhaps because of the age gap, as he was a couple of decades older. The marriage was still new when signs of struggle began to appear. They got married when I was around seven or eight, and even I could sense that something was not right. Physically they looked like a father and daughter. He was short, bald with graying hair around his ears and had a big Jewish nose. In my mind, beautiful young women marry handsome young men, like Ken and Barbie. This was not a barbie doll marriage.

Over the next few years, my family speculated she was being abused, but no one suspected the degree of violence behind closed doors. I had a hard time believing she would allow a man to harm her. A lot was hidden from me. During one of my Toronto visits, I came to realize that my family's suspicions might be correct. At ten or 11 years old, I got caught in an argument between Marja and her husband. It escalated to the threat of a hot coffee pot being thrown at his face after he'd called her a "Bitch" repeatedly. I don't recall what the fight was about, but Marja's anger was growing. I cuddled my stuffed dog, hoping to be invisible, and praying there won't be any flying coffee.

I began scouting a plan of escape, just in case, but where could I go? I'm not in my safe community of Kam anymore, and I am surrounded by millions of strangers in a strange city. Marja had warned me about big city dangers telling me, "If you have a bracelet on, cover your wrist with your jacket and wear gloves if you have rings on." At another time, she said, "Don't put your arm out the window on the bus or taxi, because someone might drive by and chop it off just to steal your jewellery." *Sisterly advice.* What kind of world did she live in?

I remember that the elevator is just around the corner. I could jump in, push L, and be taken to the lower level. This is the only place I might

go because I knew where it was. The screaming ends abruptly when he slams the office door, while Marja rubs her eyes. I stare at her for guidance, for reassurance. A fake smile appears as she says, “Don't worry, everything’s okay.” It wasn’t, but she’s the grown-up. I had no choice but to believe her.

A few years later, Marja disappeared. My parents were panic-stricken and hoped that maybe she had left her husband and was on her way home, but there was no sign of her. She had no contact with us or anyone else. I imagined she may have been mugged or kidnapped and needed rescue. Toronto was a big city, and she could be lost anywhere. There were no sightings of her, and the police began a search. Three agonizing days had passed when they finally discovered her, and we received devastating news. I was in school when the principal called me to the office. He told me a family emergency came up and I would be picked up soon. *What happened? Marja may have been found; my parents might be sick.* I didn’t know what to expect. I waited at the north exit, where I stood peeking through the door window for my ride. *This had to be bad news.*

I was unsure who was picking me up, but I kind of hoped it was my parents because then I'd know they were okay. Niina's burgundy minivan came to a stop in front of the school, and I ran down the freshly shoveled stairs, crossing my arms to stay warm. I jumped into the front seat, and she turned down the blasting heat as I hugged my packsack. Her eyes were puffy and mascara smudged. There was a small pile of tissue beside her. I took a deep breath and glanced at the empty snow-covered football field.

"What's going on?" I asked.

Quietly she said, "Marja's been found, but not alive. She passed away." The words pierced my soul. I felt the flowing blood in my body stop. Everything in the world froze; there must be a mistake.

"How… how did she die?" I asked. *Was she murdered?* The thought was too awful. Niina looked uncomfortable with my question, like she feared how I would deal with the news.

She took a deep breath and shifted her body towards me. "She committed suicide." "What! She killed herself? Are you sure?" Shock and anger boiled up inside me.

Nothing made sense. As a junior in high school, I had my own demons to fight, and had now lost Marja in a bizarre and cruel way. My beloved sister, with a fractured mind, was only 34 years old. This was to be kept a secret within our circle of relatives and friends. Society was not ready to deal with suicide. I did not ask any more questions; I didn't ask how she killed herself. I knew all about shame and secrecy, so sealing my lips would be natural.

This was an unbearably painful point for our family. I was mad and hurt; angry she freed herself from her torment, but I could not. Angry for leaving us and hurting my mom so deeply. It was a time of sorrow, confusion and many unanswered questions. *Where was she for three days? Did she leave a note?* We could not have an open casket or take pictures of the body, as our Finnish heritage does. Marja was found in the lower level of her apartment building, where she had taken me before, to swim in the pool. It was in that same place, that her suffering ended. *What thoughts and feelings ran through her mind?* I could only envision her in a time of peace when she was released from her fears and anguish. A beautiful, successful, and generous woman wasted away into nothingness. I recognized then; we shared a similar cracked mind.

Marja had lost hope and planned her escape. With many miles between her and us, no one truly knew her life on the inside, but we saw signs of struggle. We suspected an abusive marriage. We didn't understand the depth of fear she had of her husband, until years later as secrets began to unfold. *Did she end her life to break free of him?* As her body was lowered into the ground, I heard the aching cries of a mother's grief, above the quiet sobs of the crowd and the clinking noise of her wedding band, as her hand struck the casket. It felt like a final *goodbye,* and *I wish you would have just moved back home*, all in one. The sound tore up the innermost part of my heart. Nothing would ease my mom's pain of burying her third child. Weeks prior, my heart broke when I heard the news about my sister. Now seeing my mom's pain, I was mortally wounded.

I dealt with this painful experience by washing it away with liquor. My family encouraged me not to talk about her death, so there would be no making sense of such a tragedy, no sorting out what suicide means. What was her life like in recent years? Did she like being a nurse? Did she have friends? Why? - unanswered questions. Marja kept her personal life private. Her treasures, family photos, and her belongings remained with the old man, even though we tried to collect them. He refused to give us anything of hers and completely disconnected from us. I had nothing but hate for him. She left the world, and he shut us out. Not knowing how to deal with this, I self-medicated.

Chapter 18

# LAST CHANCE

In my own world, I was falling deeper into obsession, trying to hide my grief and pretending it didn't exist. No one told me how to deal with loss, and this was no ordinary death. It somehow carried a burden of shame, like our family did something to deserve this. My parents must have felt the pressure of secrecy. They had to grieve losing their daughter in private and could not focus on me. I became a stranger from my parents, disappearing days at a time.

Eventually, I moved in with a boyfriend at seventeen. I couldn't handle the rules at home and wanted freedom. Johanna and I slowly started to drift apart since our Tony trio split, and Pam became a strong presence in my life. Even though I was lost in my addiction, Pam became my rock, an anchor that I could grab onto when I was at my worst. Our close friendship resumed and weathered the boozing, self-hate, and terrible choices I made. I had no redeeming human qualities left within me, without booze.

## Box of Shame

Drunken bliss gave me courage, and I was up for anything. Teens tend to think they are invincible, and I was no exception. Death or jail; those possible consequences were nonsense to my ears. I had all this freedom on my own, I could do whatever I wanted without my parents pestering me. No one was watching over my shoulder, no nagging, or threats.

One weekend, not long after I moved out, I went to a house party with some school friends, and we drank hard, late into the night until the bottles ran dry. The house was charming and tidy, and I was glad it was a small gathering, because I didn't want to see a lovely home get destroyed. The owners vacationed in Las Vegas and left my friend Ian to house-sit. It was an uneventful evening and should have ended peacefully, but it rarely ever did. The party is not over until it's over if I had anything to say about it.

People gradually disappeared as the night went on until only a few of us were left. The half-moon shone in the night sky as we began discussing if anyone had any hidden stashes of alcohol left, but no one did. Even Trish from my English class had nothing to show. She looked intimidating with her half-shaven head and mean stare, but she was a gentle person. We often ended up at the same parties, and her obsession was weed over alcohol.

"I still have a joint left." she offered.

"I guess that's better than nothing, light 'er up." I replied. Trish's eyebrows tightened up a little at my less than enthusiastic response. We all sat outside on the deck, swaying back and forth on the patio swing sharing a joint. The nicely manicured lawn glowed from the solar lights planted along the walkway.

"There's always Leblanc's," Ian suggested.

I looked at him stunned and said, "Ian, seriously? I don't think we'd be welcomed there. As soon as we set foot on the property, we'd be ripped to shreds by the pinschers."

Leblanc's tightly guarded their family-run bootlegger operation. Their henchmen stood by the door, and Doberman pinschers circled the property. They trusted no one outside of their regular circle of customers, and we were not customers; we were high school brats. "You're right; that would never work." He agreed.

Ian sounded a bit defeated and then blurted, with his index finger in the air, "The liquor store has lots of booze."

Trish, Ian, and I stopped the swaying swing with our feet and looked at each other, knowing what Ian insinuated. A plan hatched, although not a smart one. The three of us piled into my car and headed for a late-night shopping spree. We agreed that everyone in this heist must play an equal part. If one was going down, then we'd all go down. The plan was simple, bust the glass and indulge. - a smash and grab.

The liquor store was part of a developing strip mall, but the streets were quiet during the early morning hours. A discount store was attached beside the liquor store, a bedding store, and a hair salon were on the other side. We parked by the front door, which had only one glass door and two windows. I looked around the parking lot and saw the fog rising, which made the street lights a little dimmer. My anxiety escalated, I tried to take some slow, deep breaths. My neck muscles tensed up. I was hesitating as thoughts of ending up in the slammer crossed my mind. I could barely move, but Trish and Ian were counting on me not to bail out now. I took a quick look down the street, "All clear." *It's now or never.*

“We should take our socks off and put them on our hands for protection.” Suggested Trish, as we had planned to punch the glass door.

“Good idea,” I said. Before exiting the car, we took off our socks and put them on our hands. The thick glass made it impossible to break through with our fists. We were sloppy thieves and only produced a lot of noise.

“Stand back!” Ian said. He kicked at the door and glass shattered to the ground.

We all climbed in, crunching the broken glass beneath our shoes. We were in the store. I had access to shelf after shelf of glorious liquor! I couldn’t help but have a slight grin of satisfaction, while I grabbed the biggest bottle of tequila I could find, along with some wine. We had to move fast; a passing patrol car would eventually drive by. The others filled their arms, and we were out in a flash. My beating heart hammered to the rhythm of hummingbird wings, but my driving had to appear as if we were out for a Sunday afternoon cruise to distract any suspicious eyes. The burglary was both thrilling and terrifying. Back at the house, we toasted on our successful raid.

If someone had told me when I was a young girl that this experience would be in my future, I would never have believed it. Suffering and shame changed my destiny. There was almost nothing I wouldn't do for my dear alcohol. I had to have it, even if it meant stealing it. The following days, when back in reality, guilt brewed in the pit of my stomach. The crime of burglary, destruction of property and theft, held a ten-year prison term if I was tried as an adult—a new low. The thought was terrifying and should have scared me sober, but it didn't. I kept a low profile and glued my eyes onto every police car I saw. I didn't know if there were hidden cameras or a lurking witness. In the following weeks, I noticed that security was beefed up at the store, window bars were installed, and probably an alarm system; this was all because of me. I was a criminal and the lowest dirtbag ever. I never stepped foot into the store again.

I tried to put the incident behind me, and I zipped my lips. Cops hadn't come knocking at my door, so I was safe from criminal charges. Remorse pushed me to report the crime, but the consequences terrified me. Not only by the court, but by the others involved. We made a pact, and I had to stick to it. There was honor amongst friends, over the law. That's just how it was. I had to force this into the shame box and throw away the key forever. I avoided Ian and Trish for a while, like I didn't know them. They ignored me too. It was better to stay apart and not risk talking about it. The three of us had a secret. I pushed it out of my mind, as if it didn't even happen.

I thought I'd hid my self-destruction well, but people can tell, especially sober people. My parents did not know the details, but they knew I was on a dangerous path. My mom's sensitive spirit held wisdom, and she trusted it. It never steered her wrong. Dad and I were on rocky ground. My live-in boyfriend and I were toxic together, and it only grew worse by all the drinking and fighting. It was a fast downward spiral. A few months had passed since I shared any words with Dad, then the phone rang.

"I want you to come home. That boy is trouble, and you should not be living together until you are married."

"No, Isä, I'm fine." I replied. I didn't have the energy to get into it.

"I need to see you. Can you come just to talk? No yelling."

He may have had those intentions, but he had no control over his temper. It always ended in a fight and threats of some kind. But I did agree to meet him a few blocks away from home to hear him out. *He probably won't scream if we are in the middle of the street*, I thought. I also didn't want the luxuries of home, like a decent meal and my comfy bed, to sway my revenge mission. I had a point to prove, that I'd rather live in a seedy part of town and cook canned food on a hot plate than return home. My parents must pay for taking me away from the horses and stripping away my freedom. I blamed my addiction and poor choices on them because I wasn't ready to take responsibility for my life. I was sick in my addiction.

Dad's new sky-blue Chevy S15 truck was parked ahead when I turned the corner at Faircrest Street and Frankwood Avenue. It was a 35-minute walk from the shady neighborhood where I lived, to my parent's home. The exercise kept me warm as the weather was cooling off; it was nearing November. I didn't know what to expect. His eyes looked tired and dreary, but he aged well. He had more greying hair on his head and a small old man pot belly. The past three years after Marja's death were pretty uneventful for him. He had retired from bush work and spent time visiting friends. He often shared scriptures from the bible, talking about Jesus lit his heart.

In his hand was an airmail envelope with a letter inside. We always had stacks of them because my parents wrote to their siblings in Finland. He began telling me how he wished I would move home so he would know I was okay. He told me he loved me, which were words I did not often hear, if ever. I listened and nodded to acknowledge that I heard him. Tears began to swell in his eyes, as he handed me the letter. His deepest emotions were on the page about his love for me. He described how he and Mom prayed a thousand prayers of protection over me, He'd been taking evening classes to learn to speak and write in English. The letter was written in Finn-glish - half Finnish and half English. He was putting forth a great effort to communicate with me, and I felt his vulnerability. This angry and hardened man was soft and broken at this moment, as he begged me to come home.

With love, he said, "tule kotiin Anita." My heart screamed *yes* to his invitation to return home, but my lips said, "ei," as I shook my head, took the letter, and turned my back on him. I didn't recognize this man. I'd spent most of my life on guard for his random outbursts. Now, he was open and vulnerable, tender. I felt safe around him. *Maybe he changed?* I realized that Dad had kept his promise to stay calm. *I might discuss this the next time I see him; he deserves it for his effort.*

My heart split in two, I wanted to run to him, and snuggle myself into his open arms, but I allowed arrogant pride to separate the chance of a father and daughter reconciliation. A heavy downfall of emotions streaked down my face as I walked away, trying to read his sloppy writing through my blurred vision. *I have to go home and give him a chance.* I turned the corner, and I was out of his sight. I stopped and turned around with a tiny bit of hope that he had followed me, but he didn't. He let me go. Dad was done chasing me. I would now spend the next several years chasing his ghost for a second chance.

Within weeks, he passed away at sixty-seven years old. A massive heart attack took him straight to Heaven. He died unexpectedly in church, on his birthday, just before Christmas. A birthday celebration was planned after the service, but God called him home to celebrate the milestone in Heaven. His last breaths on earth seemed fitting. Church was the center of his life, over his family. The loss was shocking, and again my mom was grief-stricken.

How does one behave or feel when losing their father? My heart split, and out poured pain, guilt, and anger that I hid from everyone. A jumbled mess of emotions and shock. Disbelief. Our family gathered at the hospital. Paramedics desperately tried to revive him, but it was too late. Upon arrival, he was gone. I was ushered to his side to say goodbye, but denial wouldn't allow me to do so. He cannot pass until I've apologized, and we have a chance to bond as he wanted.

*God, please give me one more chance!* The nurse opened the curtain, and I was alone with him. He lay on a stretcher, semi-fowlers position, in a hospital gown. His face was sunken, his eyes slightly ajar, and his lips were stripped of all color. An oropharyngeal airway was stuck in his mouth. I wanted to rip it out so he could talk. *He can't breathe with that in there! Please, I need to talk to you Isä!* I was screaming inside and hoping that this was a mistake; the doctor must be wrong, and Dad would suddenly gasp for air. I forced my tears to not escape, standing next to him, hoping for any sign of life. Nothing. My hand touched his, and the coldness made my hand flinch. This didn't seem normal, *but I am not about to say goodbye, this nightmare will end, and I'll have a second chance to talk to him*. My feet were nailed to the floor until the nurse rescued me. I sat with my family in a private room as we took turns saying goodbye. My mom was weeping in agony, and I could feel her devastation. I realized that my mom needed me now; this was my mother's time for grief, not mine.

I had to be strong for her sake; I had no choice, no more bouncing back and forth between home and boyfriends. She was now alone, and it was only logical that I would be the one to live with her. I left the terrible relationship I was in, after six months of living together, and went to my mom's side. My dad's final wish was granted. I asked God to tell my dad how sorry I was for literally worrying him to death. I didn't know if it was possible, but I vowed that my remaining parent would never leave this earth shattered because of me. Somehow, I had to make it right. I'd show him, in death, that someday I would be a good daughter. He would never hear my apology, and we would never develop a genuine relationship. The guilt crippled me, and I could not accept our time in this world had ended in this bitter, hateful place. Our last chance had passed.

The first year without Dad was a tough adjustment for all of us. Christmas came two weeks later, and we went through the motions of a family gathering. Food, gifts, and the Christmas story, which was always read by Dad; now my sister read it, as the little ones waited patiently for their presents. Explaining their Pappa's absence was as simple as, "He has gone to Heaven." I wondered how the others felt? Did they believe he was in Heaven? Did they come to closure in their adult relationship with Dad? I never did, I was robbed, and the weight of guilt pushed me further under. It was justified guilt; his heart broke one last time from his revengeful daughter, and I ran out of time to fix it. Alcohol would be the only cure.

My mom kept busy around the house with gardening and spending time with her grandkids. I had to be less focused on my misery and be supportive of her. I chauffeured Mom to the store, bank, and wherever else she wanted to go. I translated phone calls and helped around the house when I could. Together we figured out how to survive without Dad. My mom had an abundance of support from all her children, friends, and church family. The process was long, but over the years, she grew strong and independent by relying on her faith. She was in charge now, making all decisions. She escaped to camp whenever she could, enjoying life with no electricity or running water, feeding the birds, and chasing away the bears with an ax when they attempted to steal her food. The cold and the snow did not deter her camp getaways. In the winter, she snow-shoed up the long driveway, hauling her weekly supplies on a toboggan. She pushed through life's tragedies with Sisu power, and her undying faith in God kept her safe. Another life chapter had ended, and a new one began.

Sometimes we'd reminisce about Dad, but she didn't like to discuss details about his insanity. I never pushed for answers, as I knew she didn't have any. She acknowledged the dark side of Dad, and I was satisfied with that. She loved him and dealt with him the best way she could. One man was enough for her, and she blossomed into a strong independent woman. I admired her resilience but questioned my own faith. I could not let go of the pain that was coursing through my veins, which resulted in my many bad choices, including those that involved men.

Chapter 19

## FIX ME

I had broken pieces, a shattered heart, smashed spirit, and a disintegrated hope. Someone needed to sew me back together, and only a man could do that. Perhaps then, I could drink like a normal person and be happy. I could not look inward for happiness, as evil and filth dwelled there. I needed a man to fix me, and together, we could encourage each other to heal and grow. Where I saw flaws, I could fix them with love and support. I didn't realize my lack of ability to love, even with the purest of intentions.

I was still grieving when Andre came into the picture and loved me unconditionally. In no time at all, I decided that it was true love. We met at Birch Point resort. A friend of mine rented a campsite for the week, and we partied almost every night. I noticed Andre's feathered brown hair, and manly chest hairs peeking out from his black V-neck t-shirt, while he roasted a marshmallow by the fire. All eyes glued on him as he made wisecracks about his uncle's crazy life of crime. He would pause at the climax of the story and scan the faces of his audience before continuing. His facial expressions and antics would keep people at the edge of their seats. Andre was a hit with everyone, and I didn't believe he would be interested in me, but before the evening ended, he whispered sweet nothings into my ear.

We talked until the sun rose, and we learned a lot about each other's family life. His family came from Portugal in search of the American dream. They settled in the U.S. at first and then found their way to Canada. Andre's parents pressured him to go to university, but he had other plans. The new dude in the city had a growing reputation of being a tough but likeable guy. I fell under his spell of romance and devotion, even though eight years were between us. We shared some similar dysfunctions and tried to help each other heal; one wet noodle, to another. We made some headway, but it always backfired, bringing out the worst in us. Eventually, I saw a different side of him; a sneaky, cunning part. His charismatic ways convinced people to follow his ideas, including me, which seemed to stroke his ego.

Andre had a passion for guitars and worked in a small music store. The owner trusted him. He excelled and received a promotion to assistant manager rather quickly. His gift of gab and magnetism far exceeded his money management skills. He always needed more cash, and I never understood why it disappeared so fast. When he got desperate, Andre devised a plan to get some quick and easy moolah. He needed help, and he knew exactly who would become the key players in his scheme. He needed bull strength to bust open the door and an innocent-looking woman by his side, who would stand up for him on his behalf. Andre's faithful sidekick, Jeremi, who would do anything for him, did not hesitate to join in when Andre told him about the plan. Jeremi would be the real culprit who broke in, and this would be Andre's truth - he always had a scapegoat. Simple-minded and innocent Jeremi, was perfect.

Late at night, they walked to the music store, and Jeremi did as Andre told him to. His 250-pound body slammed into the door, and it flew open. Before leaving with the bag of loot, they damaged instruments and spray painted a gang-like symbol to throw off the cops. The daily cash flow had been "accidentally" left in the till instead of being deposited into the ATM as usual. He would sincerely apologize for his regrettable forgetfulness.

The next morning, the phone rang at the crack of dawn. The owner informed us about the robbery, and she wanted us both to head to the store immediately to chat with her and the police. *Why should I go? I had nothing to do with this.* Now I was getting caught in Andre's hustles. I didn't think it was fair that I would have to be involved in this chat. I'd rather turn a blind eye and let him deal with the consequences, but we got ourselves ready and walked to the store. While the police questioned Andre about the incident, the store owner asked me if I thought Andre had anything to do with it.

In his defense I said, "No ma'am, he slept beside me all night." Like a good little girl, I lied and stood by my man.

"Are you sure?" She asked suspiciously. I crossed my arms and glanced at Andre through the broken door, talking with the police inside the store. "I'm sure," I said.

Andre had me right where he wanted me, tight-lipped and on his side. After the investigation, Andre walked away a free man, which only encouraged him further. He kept denying the whole thing, but we both knew the truth. I heard jokes and innuendoes about robbing the store months before the event, but I was sure it was all just talk without action. After it happened, he said, "What an impeccable coincidence." *It sure was Andre.* Truthfully, I could not say I saw him do anything because I did sleep the whole night through. This placed a small seed of doubt in my mind. Andre denied any direct involvement but assured me that insurance would cover the owner's losses. He counted on me being voiceless, and I was.

Andre would jump at any opportunity to make money. He wasn't foolish though; he knew how to play the game without getting caught. I never saw Andre do drugs but selling them could be a profitable business. His negotiations did not occur around me, but his apartment was the hiding hut for dealers. Business was business, and the less I inquired about it, the better it was for everyone. With his mafia fantasies, I was supposed to act like the mafia wife and flush the stuff down the toilet when the cops showed up. I helped with hiding bags of marijuana in coffee tins to throw off the scent of the drug. The house was full of cocaine, hidden in the attic and the walls. Cops did occasionally visit, but Andre's slick talk and smooth demeanor distracted any possible suspicions. I sat there looking small and innocent, like I could never tell a lie.

Although I had my choice of drugs at my fingertips, alcohol remained my number one. I experimented but always turned back to my true love. Carfentanil and city-wide opioid addiction, that is now killing everyone, was not a serious issue in my day. Cocaine, acid, marijuana, and hashish were the popular highs of the 80s, but the most accessible was alcohol.

Andre's ambitions resembled those of mobsters like John Gotti or Henry Hill. His wardrobe was not only the popular acid wash jeans and rocker T-shirts, half his closet was filled with suits and ties, along with his leather jackets. He carried a briefcase for a short time, while taking a business course. He had me by his side, and a mistress on his other side. They met during his business studies, and she became his study buddy. Purely platonic, he insisted. I'm sure day one was. After-school studies eventually turned into studies of another kind - the kind that can only be done at her house. I began stalking them, driving by and sitting outside in my car, while Andre and her "studied." Andre and I had pathetic fights about it, and he chose her over me for a few weeks. When he came back apologizing and promising I was his number one girl, I welcomed him with open arms. I believed this was love, and that I was a loving partner by forgiving him.

Aside from his manipulation and cheating ways, Andre had a violent streak to those that crossed him; to those that deserved an ass-whooping. From an early age, he built his reputation, and people either loved or hated him. To the ladies, he was smooth, protective, romantic, and the comedian. This is what I fell for and needed at the time. I felt loved and cared for until our love turned into mistrust and jealousy, and it was not all on his part. As the relationship progressed, he attacked my self-worth; belittling my intelligence in front of others to build himself up. We became like poison to each other, and his dreams of a mafia family would not be in his future. His law-breaking activities eventually caught up to him, and some time behind bars allowed him to reflect on his life - hopefully he had a backup plan. It wasn't easy saying goodbye; I loved him in the only way I knew how. Pam reassured me often that I had made the right choice. Enough was enough and it was time to let go of Andre. I had no interest in a jailbird relationship, so I wished him well and moved on.

I immersed myself in finishing high school, while my peers pursued their college dreams or joined the workforce. Alcohol had replaced a semester and I did not graduate with my friends. I had huge regret for dropping out of school, came crawling back and decided to complete the required credits in one semester. That meant, a full course load of four classes, and I'd work on an extra credit at night through correspondence education. Every week my completed work was sealed in a brown envelope and snail-mailed to the distance education office. There wasn't such a thing as emailing documents.

I chose Life Management Skills for my correspondence credit and aced it! The teacher's comments glowed at how detailed my work was. My life was filled with pain, loss, mental health issues, and addiction. I clearly had no clue about how to manage life, but somehow, I'd fooled the teacher. Somewhere in the mess of Anita's being, there was some logic that I couldn't always see or trust. I surprised myself and saw that, despite all my struggles, I could reach goals when my mind was set. Where I would go from here was unknown, but I was proud of my achievement.

Since being free from Andre, I knew I should stay single. I was not ready for another relationship or capable of choosing a partner, but the destructive pattern continued. I ignored the guidance of my inner spirit; because my addiction refused to listen; I needed a boyfriend. In no time at all, I jumped into a relationship with Alex, who I knew from school. He was not my typical style. He was just a little taller than me at about five foot five, blonde and quiet. We were the same age and we hit it off; maybe he's a keeper. He was a college boy, so that's when I started to consider it for myself but had no direction in what I should study. Nursing crossed my mind, but nurses are smart, and I am not, so I gave up on that idea. I tested the waters of college life with an entry level English course and Introduction to Psychology, which I liked. The courses didn't involve multiplying or dividing, so I managed well.

I enjoyed being a student and filling my head up with nouns and verbs and learning about historical treatments for the mentally ill. I found myself in many of the psychology books I studied. As the professor spoke in front of the class, I was certain he was talking about me. My eyes would scan the students next to me to see if anyone was looking. *Could they tell if I was crazy?* I'd slouch down into my seat, trying not to make a peep as the professor talked about the traits of a psychopath, manic-depressive, schizophrenic, OCD, ADHD, and borderline personality disorder - they all fit. *Did I have a mental illness for real?* As I sat at my desk in college and learned about mental illness, it seemed as if I did. This was news that I didn't want to hear because, it would mean that I AM crazy, and there is no cure. I had no interest in traveling down this road because it would require action on my part; discussions, medications, and shock treatment? No thanks. This was far too complicated for me to accept or fix. In the meantime, alcohol was my crutch, the band-aide to hide the symptoms. Booze,

Pamela, and Mr. Perfect were all I needed to survive.

Chapter 20

# SHOCK

School helped to gain a little life perspective. My brain grew intellectually and mentally; this could be the spark I needed to get on a better track. My classes were interesting, and I had thoughts of becoming a social worker. I had compassion and acceptance to offer, but I didn't show either to myself, so supporting others would be impossible and hypocritical. However, education is never wasted. Learning was a challenge for my scrambled mind, and for once I was responsible, studying more and drinking less. This path would not last. Sadly, my college journey ended abruptly in the spring when I thought I was dying.

On an April morning, I had tossed and turned all night with an intermittent ache in my gut that slowly progressed over hours to severe cramping. I figured it must be the flu, as I hadn't been drinking. I prepared myself to miss class and spend the day in bed. By 7 a.m. it was impossible to ignore the extreme pulses, and I had to get to the bathroom. I took a few steps clutching my stomach and left my bedroom, then crouched to the floor on my hands and knees - I have another fifteen feet to go and the pain intensified. Aching, throbbing, stabbing; this had to be the C-word. People talked about how excruciating dying from cancer was, so this must be it. The muscle cramp in my belly intensified and the pain traveled throughout my entire body, pulsing. The basement floor was damp and musty. I collapsed onto my side to try and ease the jabs, then crawled closer to the door. My mind was racing as I inched my way closer to the bathroom, now just ahead of me. The pink rug was in view through the open door. I was near, yet still, so far - the trek may as well be a mile long. My strength dwindled and every movement was excruciating. I'd never been this near to death before and I was terrified. Teardrops landed on the concrete as I prayed for God to get me out of the house. I did not want my mom to find me dead on the floor, with no clue about what happened.

The bathroom entrance was finally within reach, and I grabbed a hold of the sink to pull myself up. A peculiar gush and plop landed in the toilet, and the aching subsided. I did not understand what happened, but with less pain, I could walk upright again. I looked down into the bowl and saw a plum-sized tumor floating around the red sea of blood. After a quick wash, I threw on some sweats, grabbed my jacket and dashed out the back door, trying to avoid a conversation with my mom. Just minutes before, I faced death and experienced the worst agonizing affliction ever, and now I might survive. I had no idea what had occurred, but I was pain-free.

I considered going to class as normal because the suffering dulled, but instead I drove to Alex's house, and his parents saw that I was sick. My face looked pale and tired, but I didn't want to discuss what just happened because I was not comfortable talking about these details with Alex; we'd only dated for a few months. I didn't know him well enough to talk about womanly issues. I preferred to relax and fully recover from whatever death plague had tried to get me. I sipped some water and rested on the couch for a moment, until the torture began again. His parents immediately told me to go to the hospital, so I reluctantly agreed. The fear of being diagnosed with a terminal illness made me want to stay away from the hospital, but I knew it was the right thing to do. I took a brief bathroom break to pull myself together before we went.

The pain became unbearable again and my mind was lost. Somehow my body took over my mind, and knew what to do. I removed my pants, stepped into the tub, and ran some warm water to drown out the sound of my sobs. There was a knock at the door, as I groaned in agony. My gut felt like it was being violently stabbed by a thousand knives. *This is punishment for my sins.* My hands grasped the side of the claw tub, my head fell back, and my teeth crunched together like a vice grip. My voice whimpered like a dying dog as I searched for Heaven, remembering Jesus in my living room when I was a little girl. *He last told me that it was not my time, but this must be my time*. I couldn't see him yet, but I was accepting the inevitable. My entire torso clenched, hard as a rock, and I couldn't imagine why.

Suddenly, a heavy clunk lands beneath me, and the stabbing ceases—finally, relief. My muscles relax, I sit on my knees, and I can exhale. Blood swims towards the drain and beneath me is a peculiar sight of what looked like a miniature doll, but I didn't understand how it got there. I place the tiny four-inch body in my palm, tracing the face with my thumb, etching the skeletal curves of a nose and cheekbones into memory - I am holding a person in my hand. Possibly a future doctor, artist or an astronaut, only God knows. A human life had grown in secret. Did this mean I was pregnant? The messaging system between eyesight and brain is severed. A lifeless being somehow grew and died in darkness. I feel lost in space somewhere, just a shell of skin and my senses are gone. My vision is hazy, but the door is open and hits the wall - I hear nothing. It takes hours for my boyfriend to leap two steps towards me. "Sheee neeeeds toooo geeet tooo theee hooospitaaal nooow!" *I think he said I need to go to the hospital.* He scoops me up and rushes to a nearby hospital, and I spend the day there getting ultrasounds, blood work, and recovering from shock. The nurse asks me for the baby, but through the trauma, I did not think to bring it. They estimate that I was in my second trimester.

In hindsight, the signs were there, but my hormones did not function properly due to my childhood traumas. While most girls experienced their periods before age thirteen, mine came at age 15; I had STIs (sexually transmitted infection) by then. The health care professionals knew I was living a high-risk lifestyle that could affect my fertility later in life. Motherhood could possibly never have a page in the books for me. The news was devastating, and the future grew darker and darker. With a family of my own out of the picture, I saw no need for birth control.

Some time had passed before being able to process the loss of my baby. I distanced myself from Alex, because my pain was too deep. We were a new couple and not able to deal with the loss. Eventually, reality sunk in, and I realized I had been pregnant and in labor for hours. How could I have not known? I longed for this child in my arms and to be called a mommy. I told myself if only I'd known I was pregnant, I would have stopped drinking. However, my addiction was so severe, maintaining sobriety would've been impossible. Pam did her best to listen while I tried to talk about my experience, although she'd never been through this kind of trauma. Her empathy and open ear made a difference. *Someone in the world cares*. I mourned and longed for my infant. Nothing is worse than the loss of a child. After the trauma, I could not return to college, the guilt swallowed me up. I killed my own flesh and blood with alcohol. I blamed myself for the baby's death, even though I didn't know he/she existed. I did the only thing I knew how to do: drink myself silly.

I was drinking rum and Crown Royal whisky at the time, only because it was available. I never understood why people chose this beverage over that. My only mission was to have the drink with the highest alcohol content or whatever I could get my hands on. I saw no point in getting a little tipsy; I wanted to reach a complete drunken bliss, and escape reality. I will admit that those summer coolers tasted great, like juice with a twist. One or two did nothing, but a dozen might get me there if I didn't puke first from the sweetness.

I had sunk further into desperation and had a new crowd to hang with. We shared the same vision, drink into insanity. We all blubbered out our tears one minute, then laughed like maniacs the next. The nights would involve fighting at some point and blackouts. Sometimes, blood would spill and to the ER we'd go. Together we'd support each other emotionally and physically, regardless of who it was. I was known as the "Finn Fish," meaning I was Finnish, and my mouth was always open, gulping alcohol. Tom was the crazy native kid, short and scrappy; he protected us. Shane, my good pal, was the mediator; he kept me alive and knew when to stop drinking. Someone in the bunch needed to have some sense.

Shannon was a friend of Tom's and a lady of the night. She was a short blonde-haired girl working in the East end. One night she showed up at our door with a bloody face and her white thigh highs torn to pieces. She needed help, so my friend and I brought her to the hospital. She walked with a limp in her cowboy boots and threw her purse onto the row of chairs in the emergency department. She then swung up her injured leg and rested it on a bench. The look of paranoia and irritation was on her face. Winter had not yet arrived, but she wore a bomber-style white fur jacket and a short jean skirt. The coat was beautiful, and I wished I was brave enough to wear something so lavish. As we sat in the waiting room, I wondered how she became a prostitute. I wondered if she had a family or ran away from home. She was so pretty and brave and could be great at life. I saw an abundance of hope in others, but I, myself, was hopeless and undeserving.

I asked her, “What happened?”

She said nonchalantly, “honey, it’s a workplace hazard.”

She lived her life on the edge. My way of life was similar, but I didn’t get paid. Family men and grandpas trolled the streets for young flesh all the time, and there would be no shortage of customers, if I’d chosen that path. Late one night, while I was walking down a dark street, a man in a grey Lincoln car pulled up behind me.

He opened the black, powered window and asked, “Are you working tonight?” *Working? Does it look like I am at 3 a.m. on the street? Oh, wait a minute, he’s asking if I’m tricking!*

I picked up my pace and said, “No, I’m not working.”

"I have a lot of money. It's yours if ya want it," he replied while rubbing his index finger against his thumb.

I looked away and kept walking while my ears listened for the sound of shifting gears, to make sure he disappeared into the night. He slowly crept past me and turned down the next street. I filed away that career choice for now. As long as the drinks were coming to me, I didn't need to go there.

*A workplace hazard.* I wondered if she told the truth about her injuries. Maybe they'd seen her there before. She got released with a fractured nose and a prescription for pain pills. Throughout the years, I often wondered where life had taken her. Did she escape those terrible years we were living? Did she find hope and recovery? Maybe she is forever 18? That night was the last I ever saw of her.

Chapter 21

## COMPETITION CRAZY

My body had developed a tolerance for alcohol, and I out-drank a lot of people. I could slam back beers and shots all night without passing out or vomiting, which was impressive, considering my small stature - life goals at this stage. I had finally found my drinking match. Like me, Randy was a seasoned drunk and impressed with how much of a lush I was. He lived in a neighborhood of old rundown houses, with a mix of young neighbors and elderly. Some had resided there for over 50 years. Bars, restaurants, and grocery stores were all within walking distance. Randy's street had the odd renovated house that modernized the area, but his house had never been updated. It had old, weathered siding that was falling off in some parts. The door to the front porch had flakes of paint missing, and black garbage bags were duct-taped over shattered windows in the front; drunken rages were the cause. The cold exterior was meant to keep visitors away. It looked more like a haunted house. I'm sure if the walls could talk, they would whisper haunting secrets of family traumas.

The home was a tall, skinny two-floor structure owned by his mother, but she did not live there. It seemed she may have lost control of her home and left. Her children basically overtook the home. The sex, drugs and rock-and-roll lifestyle were not a part of her senior days. On my first visit to Randy's, he warned me to keep my shoes on. I thought perhaps the floors hadn't been mopped in awhile, so I did as he said and followed him upstairs. Musty, rotten smells of feces smacked my nostrils before I got to the upper level. The living room floor was covered in several piles of dog crap. The home hadn't been mopped or swept for quite some time. I didn't consider myself a neat freak or germaphobe by any means, but this was too much. I was speechless, as I carefully tiptoed my way over to a kitchen chair that seemed clean enough to sit on. Empty beer bottles lined the counters and ashtrays were always full of butts. Garbage was scattered here and there, empty pizza boxes or piled up flyers. Dirty dishes sat in the sink with hardened food stains. Eventually, someone would soak them overnight before washing them. An appetite was killed quickly by the hideous stench in the air, and cooking was not a priority. The dark hallway had a shelf and a row of boxes filled with stuff that would one day be organized, but it never was. The place needed a thorough decluttering and sanitizing job.

This was my introduction to my boyfriend's life, and I didn't run.

On weekends I would stay there but would spend most of my time downstairs in Randy's room. His sister and her boyfriend hung out upstairs with the Rottweiler. I slept in a single bed with Randy in his cluttered room. A small bar fridge was next to his bed with cold Bud Lites in it, and this also served as a bedside table. Sand and grit from the un-swept floor, constantly covered the bedsheets. I tried whisking it away, but it was always there. Randy didn't seem to notice it, so I learned to ignore the dirty sheets, and it became a normal part of our lives. The messy surroundings became invisible. People sat on the couch every day, slamming beers and snorting lines. I had the freedom to do as I pleased here. I had access to alcohol and attention from a man. I could ignore the hideous smells, and once I passed out, I didn't feel the sandy sheets.

Randy was not the type of guy you bring home to mom and he knew this. He was empty, suffered from depression, self-esteem issues, and internal turmoil. Social situations without beer made him uncomfortable, and his circle was small. He would only allow a few people into his depressing world. I was one, and together we made it through life in an abnormal twisted way. My mental health problems were similar, but our environments were very different. I casually told Pam about him but left out some details. She didn't need to know that I stepped around dog crap or that I slept in the dingy room of filth. The truth is, I knew she would want me to leave him, and I didn't want to hear it. She'd tell me I deserved someone much better. She was right, but I was not ready to believe it.

When Randy and I ventured out, it would usually be when the sun went down. We often hung out at a small sports bar nearby, playing pool and drinking cheap pitchers of beer. Randy loved making people laugh with his cheesy jokes, one of his favorites was, *"A horse walks into a bar and the bartender asks, 'Why the long face?"* He thought it was hilarious, and he'd laugh like crazy. His goofy humor drew me to him, as well as his waist-long, dark hair that he sometimes wore in a ponytail. He often "joked" about offing himself with a shotgun or hanging himself. I never knew how to take it because he'd laugh immediately after making that comment. We both behaved in behaviors for the pure shock value.

After a few dozen beers between us, our nights of laughter would usually end in a fistfight.

We fought as hard as we drank. Sometimes I'd have to cake on the make-up and wear sunglasses, but I still did not see anything wrong with this. Randy would be the one to blame if people saw my face, but I felt like an equal. He hit me, and I hit him back - I'd do the same if he were a female. The more we drank, the more insane we became. It was a lifestyle I never envisioned for myself.

One day, Randy wanted to show me how he could slide down the handrail of the stairs. He sat on the banister at the top and began his descent, midway down, he lost his balance and flipped over the rail, crashing into a metal shelving unit. We headed straight to the emergency department with a few injuries and a possible broken wrist. We were scrapping at the hospital, about how dumb he was to attempt such a stunt, behind the curtain wall in one of the rooms.

"How can you be so stupid? Now we're gonna be stuck here all night!" I yelled.

"Shut the fuck up! I didn't plan on breaking my wrist!" *SMACK!* I walloped him right across the face. I was there to support him, his reckless moves were taking up my time, and this is how he treats me. I was furious!

He grabbed my arm and squeezed. "You psycho! Don't fucken start here!" I glared into his eyes, my face in front of his and whispered, "Psycho? I'll show you fucken psycho!"

I yanked my arm away from him and stormed out to the parking lot and sat in my car, with my heart racing. Frustration and anger were building up and I needed release. I smacked the steering wheel with both hands sputtering out vulgar words, thinking about how to vent. I didn't have a baseball bat, so I couldn't thrash the car, but I could still do damage. I spotted the cigarette lighter on the console and pushed it in, within seconds the lighter popped out. The circular coils inside were burning hot and ready for the tip of a cigarette, but my need for escape was overwhelming and I wouldn't use it to smoke. A verbal argument in the hospital, ended in a warped dysfunctional competition about who's crazier. *No one is crazier than me*. I slammed the lighter straight down onto the bare skin on my thigh, lifted it and did it three more times, scorching my skin. This was the release I needed, and self-harm was not new to me. The first scorch was for Ronnie taking away my innocence; the second for my parents, for taking me away from my country home and freedom; the third was for my sister's death and secret baby; the fourth scorch was for the heavy guilt I carried about my dad's death. Above all, I blamed my behavior on Randy for making me mad and forcing me to act out.

I was finally satisfied and lit a cigarette with the same lighter, inhaled, and blew the smoke out the car window into the warm air. After momentarily releasing my anxiety, the red circles on my thigh started to blister, and the stinging became unbearable. As my eyes filled with tears, I left the car and walked back into the hospital, trying to pull down my jean shorts to cover what I'd done. I stood by the triage desk and asked to see a doctor. "For what purpose?" Asked the nurse. I immediately broke away from her eye contact because I couldn't express why. The fear of her finding out how I'd received the injuries, made me want to leave, but my burned leg is beginning to feel like torture.

"Can I just see a doctor; my leg is hurt."

"How did your leg get injured?" My eyes were glossy, and my breathing had become rapid. *Why can't I just see a doctor? I'd rather not talk about it more than I had to.*

"I don't know!" I said as I dropped my head onto the counter. "Please, I need a doctor." I begged. She gave up on getting any details and told me to have a seat.

I waited a while, ended up next to Randy as a patient, waiting for treatment on second and third-degree burns, and was interrogated about how I received the injuries. Randy had a different nurse from me, and my nurse just came on shift, so she hadn't witnessed our argument. I'm not sure if she knew we were a couple, and I didn't want her to know. While she wrapped my leg, she asked, "did someone do this to you?" I looked down at the floor, ignoring her. "It's alright." she said. "I just want to make sure you're safe when you leave here." *Did she think I was not safe? Was she planning on keeping me here, locking me up in the looney bin?* I did not understand what she meant, but if she thought I was not safe, would the cops be called? Would there be questioning and threats towards Randy or me? And most importantly, would rehab or counseling be forced on me?

These thoughts made me panic. There was no way in hell I was going to stop drinking! I had to act calm, seem as normal as possible, and hope that she would believe that the burns were an accident, even though, I couldn't come up with a plausible scenario.

I scanned the room through the cracked curtains. Randy had gone for an X-Ray. Every bed in the place was occupied. Worried parents cradled their sick babies, and a wrinkled little lady on a stretcher stared at me, mouthing words I couldn't hear. Opposite the row of beds, was the nursing station. I looked for the psychiatric ward, but I didn't see it. I remained tight-lipped about the incident and played the game of distraction, whenever the nurse asked about my leg. Randy's wrist ended up in a splint and we headed out - he gave me a smirk, "You're fuckin' nuts," he said with a look of pride. I looked at him, shrugged my shoulders, and smiled as we walked to the car. "Actually, you're psychotic."

His smirk changed to a look of confusion. Panic stirred in my gut. *Did I take it too far? Did I push him away?* I needed him; I better calm down on the crazy. What level of psychotic behavior is appropriate? Like a chameleon, I adapted to my surroundings to please him. I felt ridiculous about the stunt and now had to hide this huge dressing wrapped around my thigh.

Every third day a nurse had to change the dressing, and I silently screamed from the torture of the treatment. Throughout the summers, I always wore shorts, but now had to wear long loose pants to disguise my wounded leg. My mom was happy to see me covering my legs for a change, so she didn't ask any questions. Eventually, a small sterile pad replaced the massive ones, and I could change it myself. The nurses continued to try to get answers from me about how I got burned, but I would never tell a soul the truth. Several months passed before I healed, but the scars remained. When I got questioned about my leg, I had to make up a story, otherwise, people sometimes got the impression that my boyfriend had done this to me; like he tortured me. The questioning always made me squirm. What sounded worse*? "Yes, Randy scorched me,"* which is a terrible lie to say about someone or *"I did this to myself, I'm bat shit crazy!"* Either scenario sounded completely horrible, and I tried to avoid this conversation with people at all costs.

It seemed clear that my brain had dysfunction. A part of me knew I was making terrible choices, but the consequences did not scare me enough. I was a lost soul coasting in a world that I didn't belong in. I felt hopeless like no one cared. Randy's perspective was the same; our abnormal bond could not be understood. I did not try to explain him to anyone. I kept him as my secret boyfriend for ten months. So, when I fell off the face of the earth, red flags flapped in front of Pam.

Chapter 22

# KEEP RUNNING

I was scheduled to work at my banquet waitressing job on Friday. Pam and I worked together, and she was now renting a room in my basement to experience some independence away from her parents, while still being safe under my mom's roof. Jari completed school, moved out again, and was working as a nurse in a psychiatric hospital, so Pam rented his room. My mom charged her a small monthly fee, and Pam was thrilled to have her own room next to mine. We were both nineteen years old at the time. Friday came and I was a no show. With us being friends, roommates and co-workers, my sudden absence caused concern for Pam. I left without a word to her.

On the day I abandoned my life, I convinced my mom I was going on an extended trip, and I'd call her in a few days. She was still learning how to be a widow, and at my age, she didn't have a say in my decisions. If I kept Mom informed just enough, she would keep things quiet, and I wouldn't have to worry about being found by the cops or my siblings. I just wanted to drink myself to death in peace. Pam could not be fooled because she knew truths about me, ugly ones. She knew I was not on vacation and that I was up to no good. I did not say one word about it to her because I thought it would hurt her.

The fact is, I had no reasonable explanation about why I was running away with an abusive drunk. I was running from pain, grief, and from myself. She heard bits and pieces of information from friends, and my mom could confirm the city I was in but knew nothing else. Although Pam did not know Randy, she knew he was bad news. She tried but did not understand how much turmoil I carried inside, and there was nothing she could do. Pam's only wish was that I would have at least said good-bye, by any means. Instead, I turned my back on my world and her, leaving without two simple words. I did not trust her enough to face her, and it broke her heart. She did not know, nor did anyone, if I'd ever return.

My bag was packed early on a Friday morning. Randy's friends invited us to move to Sault Ste. Marie, Ontario. They had made the move just a couple of months prior and wanted company. This could be just what we needed, a change of scenery, away from judging eyes. Without much thought, we skipped town to get a fresh start in a city we'd never been to. Not many people knew about our plans. After an eight-hour drive, we arrived in the Soo (the city's nickname) and bunked at our friend's house until we could find a place of our own. Within a few days, I called my mom to tell her I was safe and sound, but I couldn't talk to Pam; I was too ashamed about how I left.

It didn't take long to find a top-floor apartment, on Wellington Street, which was close to the downtown area. I was surprised we secured it, considering we had no money or jobs. The small apartment had a few basic furnishings, and it sweltered in the summer. Our neighbors on the main floor, an elderly couple, would sometimes bang the walls when they'd heard enough of our fights, which only made our screaming louder. To clear my head, I would walk to a nearby park with a large water fountain, sprinkling the sounds of nature. Water would squirt from the center of a birdbath onto a circle of rocks and greenery. It would cascade into a shallow basin of water, edged with concrete seating. The area had many businesses, bars, and restaurants, which we mostly avoided. From the park, I could see a few narrow streets with high, broken fences and some abandoned houses, and random shopping carts were strewn about. The Park had a few lamp posts and shrubbery nearby. I would rest in my thoughts, undisturbed for a few minutes.

If I had a penny, I would've made a wish to be cantering on Future, on the beach, floating on her back. I missed the horses and Johanna. Johanna had also left Thunder Bay to explore and become herself, as she traveled alone to Western Canada. We were both lost in our separate worlds, yet somehow connected even though we did not speak for years. We would never have those times back; they were distant memories from a lifetime ago that I longed for. Time machines only existed in my imagination and returning would never be possible.

Getting a job in a strange city terrified me. The new environment was enough of an adjustment, and I didn't have the energy or focus to make decisions. We had no cash, and I waited for an eviction notice to be taped onto our door. Drinks in exchange for some chit-chat and laughs were easy but coming up with rent money was a different story. What could I do?

My mom was very wise with her funds. She stretched every penny to provide for our needs but did not fulfill all our wants. Dad's wallet was not as tight; he sometimes bought me things on our trips to town that Mom would not have approved. An afternoon lunch at McDonalds, a 10k gold pinky ring, and a Native American beaded necklace were some of the treasures. But the lesson I carried with me from both parents was that working for a paycheck provides for your needs and wants. We never accepted money from anyone, even at times when it was needed.

When my parents and their half dozen children came to Canada, they were given a small government grant to feed and clothe the family for a short time; that's how it worked with foreigners entering Canada. They viewed it as a loan and graciously accepted the money, knowing they planned to pay it back someday, even though they didn't have to - they wouldn't take a handout. I'm sure, because of the language barrier, they didn't understand how the Canadian government worked. When finances improved, they paid back every penny of the free grant.

I thought of this as I stepped into the Social Services office to apply for welfare. Rent was due, the cupboards were empty, and my mind was disabled. I swallowed what pride I had left and explained that I'd just moved to town and needed help while I looked for work. I lied about the looking for work part. The first check came, and the cash covered a few basics before I canceled the whole thing completely, because I was ashamed that I accepted the money. I *should* be able to work. Why was it so challenging to put myself out there?

Physically I looked capable of working. I had no limitations, but mentally, I was ill. Mental illness was something I was not ready to reveal. There had to be a Plan B. Hooking? Panhandling? Robbing a bank? Thankfully, I would skip Plan B because Randy found a job in a restaurant doing what he loved to do: cook. The pay was low, but it almost covered the bills, and he could steal food from the restaurant so we'd have booze money.

I was isolated and drowning my pain in alcohol. I was extremely lonely. The pressures of life weighed heavily on us, and the relationship spiraled further down into darkness. As our frustrations and drinking deepened, our fighting escalated. Communicating honest words did not come easily to either of us. Somehow, after a nasty verbal or physical fight, we felt relief. The fighting continued and eventually reached a point of no return. Randy's blows got harder, and it no longer seemed like an equal battle. He loomed over me and was a hundred pounds heavier, but I never feared him until now. I never backed down from a fight, but something was different this time: this giant was going to take me down.

The final showdown came in an intense screaming match in the kitchen. I was less combative because I'd never seen his fury like this before. His angry words were sputtering all over me and before I realized the gravity of the danger, he lunged towards me, thrusting my body into the air before it hit the wall. I dropped to the floor like a sack of potatoes and stars filled my peripheral vision. It took a moment before my vision stabilized, and I saw the staircase to freedom on my left, but I couldn't get there. Randy snatched a steak knife from the table and picked me up from the floor by my hair. *I have to get out of here before he kills me but I'm too terrified to move.* The knife presses against my throat, his body pushed against me, suffocating my lungs.

His normally puffy pale face was glossy and red, inches from mine, with fire in his eyes and rage in his soul. His breath expelled a gross scent of cheap beer and cigarettes. My head was well secured in his grip by a fist full of my hair, one good twist and my neck would snap. I didn't dare move a muscle. The place looked like a crime scene with my body imprinted in the wall and kitchen chairs toppled over, only no blood splatter yet.

He spewed out nasty words, "You do know how easy it would be for me to kill you, right… RIGHT!?" He bounced my head against the wall when I failed to answer quick enough. "I could slice this knife from here to here and watch you fucking bleed to death." The serrated edge of the blade, scratched my throat from one side to the other. In a whisper, I agreed. Randy would get no argument from me, no matter what he said. My plan was to keep him calm, so he wouldn't start slicing. I was focused and had decided that I am going to live, and when I make a firm decision, nothing stops me. I will force life onto me; there was no way in hell I would be featured on the morning news as a victim of domestic abuse!

I stay focused, docile, and hope he is satisfied in the terror he is inflicting upon me. I scan the room and see the fire escape ahead of me. To my right, the living room entrance, where I can jump out the window, but it's a long drop. My legs would break from the fall, but my screams might get the attention from the neighbors, and I'd be saved. I wait and wait. The one split second comes for a decision. *Act now!* I let him think I surrendered, that he won, by relaxing my body. His grip loosens when he feels my limp muscles, I suddenly spring out of his grasp and make a dash for the fire escape. I soar over the broken kitchen chair in one leap and bolt down the narrow stairs along the building. I run into the night, never once looking back in fear that it may slow me down.

## Box of Shame

My only thought is, *don't look back, keep your eyes in front of you, so you don't trip. Keep running!* Adrenalin fills my legs; my heart is a machine, and the green flag drops - I can outrun a bullet at this speed. The streets are empty and people are tucked away in their beds, safe and sound. I'm alone, in darkness, running away from the bad guy again. I have no idea where I'm going, then spot a bright 7-Eleven sign a few blocks ahead. In a crazed mess, I fling open the door, not noticing if there were customers in the store. A teenage boy, close to my age, stands behind the cash register, scanning me from top to bottom. I am breathless, have a thin laceration on my neck, and I'm sure a look of terror on my face. "I need to hide!" I pant for breath. I am practically halfway over the counter when he stops me.

"Hey, you can't come back here!" His eyes pop in surprise. "Do you want me to call the cops?" He picks up the phone and dials 9...

"NO… STOP, gaaawd, don't call 911! If you call the cops, I'm dead!" I said. "My boyfriend just tried to kill me, and he might be looking for me now. Please let me hideout for just a few minutes. I'll be really quiet, I promise."

*What would I do if he forced me out onto the street? I didn't know where Randy was.* Finally, I convinced him to put down the phone and hide me. I sat on the floor trying to smooth out the nest of hair on my head, what was left of it. I pushed myself against the counter as far as possible, quivering like a scared mouse, flinching every time the door opened. A few customers came and went, then Randy walked in - my breathing stopped. I leaned further back so he couldn't spot me if he looked over the counter.

Standing near the cash register, he asks, "Have you seen a short blonde girl come in here tonight?"

"No, it's been a quiet night." Says the teenager.

I am relieved that he doesn't give me up. Randy stays for a minute longer. I am a statue, even though I'm shaking on the inside, I'd learned how to survive maniacs, so my body knows what to do. I bow my head, close my eyes and try to determine his next move.

"Ok, thanks," Randy says, as I hear his steps fade away and exit the store.

The store clerk looks down at me on the floor. "You really need to get out. I can't have this kind of shit going on here while I'm working."

"Please, just another few minutes," I begged.

He rolls his eyes and leaves the counter area to go stare out the window. I stay in my position until my nerves have settled, and I ask him to use the phone. I call the only people I know in the city, our mutual friends. They agree to hide me temporarily. I thank the clerk and slip out the back door.

I discussed vague details about our fight with the mutual acquaintances, but they could see by my neck that it was a violent one. They told me Randy had been there, upset that I'd run away from him. He likely wouldn't return, so I could be safe, for now, and I definitely did not want to get the cops involved; this may lead to charges, court, and testifying. I was weak and again felt the sting of being blamed for Randy's actions. I didn't feel safe facing authorities. They didn't like kids like me, alcoholics, and troublemakers.

A few days is all it took to collect myself and, I arranged to go back home to Thunder Bay. Our friend's phone would sometimes ring with Randy's voice on the other end. He assumed I was there, which I was, but they lied on my behalf, to which I am forever grateful. Randy told them he had completely blacked out and had no memory of the night - I didn't care. I left, and I never saw him again. The whole nightmare stayed in my rear-view mirror.

Chapter 23

# DEFEATED

Family and friends welcomed me home. My mom was relieved to have me in her sights again. I did not tell anyone about how close to death I'd come. My body, mind and spirit were exhausted. I needed rest and to surround myself with familiarity. I reconnected with Pam. She was my constant, always standing by my side, even when I shut her out. Her wisdom was beyond her years and her love for me never faltered. Quietly she hoped and prayed that my self-annihilation would stop before it was too late. In her eyes, I had beauty and great potential. When I looked in the mirror, emptiness and failure were all I saw.

Things began to change direction in a subtle way. Even my dreams, which were often vivid nightmares, began to shift towards pleasant scenes. I started having dreams where I was sober and loving alcohol-free living, enjoying the sunrise, content while interacting with people. Perhaps this was a sign of things to come. Something in my mind was transforming, and I felt a genuine glimpse of hope. I had support from a small circle of loved ones. When I couldn't see that I was worthy enough to live, others believed it for me and prayed for protection and freedom. I tried to believe life could be different, and a brighter future was ahead. Crazier things had happened.

I managed to get a job as a cleaner in a sauna establishment where my mom worked. She was thrilled to have me as a co-worker. I worked part-time and contemplated school again. It was a job away from customer service, so I thought I might be able to handle it for a while. I checked into college courses and enrolled in an office administration program. It was not a suitable career choice but, considering my poor decision-making skills up to this point, I'd say going to college for *anything* was a step in the right direction. A desk job never crossed my mind before, but I chose education instead of wasting my existence away. Maybe a quiet office job would keep me out of trouble. A few months went by, and I participated in life like a big girl. Two semesters flew by and summer was approaching. Pam was getting married in the fall, and I immersed myself into her joy, fulfilling my Maid of Honor duties. During this period, I met my future husband Gary, the brother of the groom, and best man in the wedding party. The family seemed very nice and invited me for Thanksgiving dinner.

Gary and I were swept into a whirlwind romance and things moved swiftly. I fell in love with a hard-working, decent guy, although he came with a catch; he didn't drink. He had three years of sobriety under his belt, which trumped all, including girlfriends, and I knew this from the start. Would I fit into his world? He knew I drank, but he never knew the severity of my alcoholism. I made him believe that it wasn't that bad, that I was a social drinker and didn't use drugs, so I was okay.

Over the years, I convinced myself that I had control over the addiction. After all, I was not a junkie or a stoner, my drug was legal, and that somehow made all the difference. Druggies were the wild ones, and I wasn't addicted to drugs. I hadn't realized yet that alcohol was, in fact, a drug and I was highly addicted. Alcoholics will justify their actions to keep drinking. I was no more or less of an addict just because I did not choose to inject or snort drugs. Gary learned these lessons with his recovery journey, so I couldn't pull the wool over his eyes for long. He knew the lies alcoholics tell themselves and others. The relationship was new, so if my drinking began to disrupt his sober life, he would walk away. Marriage was not on the table at this early stage, so ending it would've been easy.

I decided I would keep both worlds; a man who wouldn't lay a finger on me and the occasional night of getting hammered. Limiting my binges was not difficult to do when life was smooth sailing. I believed I had control over alcohol because I had many sober nights since meeting Gary. By willpower alone, I reigned over the addiction that caused turmoil over my life, for a time. After nine months of dating, I moved in with Gary. My nights of getting sloshed became much harder to hide. My willpower began failing me. I refused to stash alcohol in the home because Gary worked for his sobriety - I would be respectful of that. My drinking could only be away from our home.

Life overall was much calmer and death-defying chaos didn't seem to find me as it used to. However, my insecurities and insanity still crept in - our relationship was tested. I didn't know how to connect to people, especially men. I was in transition of letting go of the old me but did not know how to be anything different. I pushed Gary's buttons, challenging him. *How far into anger can he go before he loses all control?* I played the mind games of a fourteen-year-old girl. I had chronic depression and poor self-worth. One minute we loved each other like mad, the next we were full of hate, but our love was deep, and it overpowered hatred. Finally, I met someone who came out of alcoholism and lived to speak about it, perhaps I could do that too. Months passed and the roller coaster continued. Gary and I were bonding on a deeper level, a friendship blossomed with my mom, and I found myself opening up to her about my struggles. We were working our way back to each other, which was a chance I never had with my dad. It felt good to be on a better path, but I still lived in my dual life, and it was causing problems. Drunken nights always ended in disaster, even though they occurred less often.

At seven a.m. one morning, I nearly killed the driver of a compact red car on the highway. Gary travelled up north for work during the week, so this was the perfect opportunity for a bender. I lived in an alcohol-free zone, so I had to drive to town for some booze. A twelve-pack and a 40-ouncer of vodka should do it. Since I didn't drink as often, I would make it count.

The binge began at home until I got lonely and bored, then I needed excitement. I drove back to town and found an old drinking buddy. We lounged on her couch and, walked the city in the darkness until dawn, hours had passed. I was tired but thought I must be sober enough to operate a vehicle, but just in case, I snuck through quiet suburban streets to the highway. I'd be safe from the cops now, there wasn't much traffic, and the sunrise not yet in full bloom. I cruised in our 1989 Chevy truck, eager to pass out in my bed.

My foot accelerated the gas petal as I rounded the last corner before home, veering into the other lane. A car appeared out of nowhere directly in front of me. With a second to spare, he swerved towards the ditch; tires squealed on the pavement. My hands braced the steering wheel and my elbows deadlocked as I stomped on the brake to pull over; an inch further, and it could've been a double fatality. I exhaled and began to breathe again, my body shuddered at the thought that my drinking almost caused a disaster. Death, DUI, jail, exposing my secret life, were all catastrophes I just narrowly avoided. I had things to lose at this point, and, I wanted to live. Mom and I were tight, Gary was in my life, new faces in recovery were entering my world, and my past acquaintances had forgotten about me. This was the start of a life that I didn't want to give up. Drinking was the problem and I had to do something about it. I finally accepted that I was an alcoholic.

Glancing behind me, I saw a cloud of dust and taillights fading away. The driver regained control and disappeared. I'd never tell Gary about this awful night, when I almost killed someone, or myself, how I almost destroyed his Chevy, how I was so plastered from supper time until seven in the morning, or how disgusted with myself I was. He would never hear the truth.

The truck crawled down the highway at turtle speed. I focused on the only thing I could see, the yellow line, because home was just around the bend. Somehow, a shield of protection surrounded me that day and I prayed to God *if I made it back alive, I'd never touch another drop again.* Fortunately, no one died during my drinking career. Juggling two lives got exhausting and proving that I could be a social drinker became impossible. I'd known this for awhile but could not admit it. I'd met other people who lived without booze, so surely it had to be possible. Normal is what I longed for, but I would never have it. I'd have to be something else. The social drinkers club was not for me. I stood at the crossroad. I would either walk away from Gary and back into my comfortable boozing madness, or I would step out of my comfort zone and live sober.

The years of wild inebriated nights scrolled through my head, and I realized what I must do. My views changed, in part, from listening to Gary's road to recovery. I felt as if my life had been spared dozens of times for a greater purpose. I felt like I would run out of chances soon; like I was on my last life. I didn't know what the future held beyond that first day, but life was going to be different. I stopped planning my next binge and stopped concocting lies. Alcohol was the enemy and, I considered it a severe allergy that would kill me or someone else - I wasn't wrong. It had filled in the emptiness on my behalf for nine years, and now the pattern had to change. What would fulfill me? How do I keep away painful memories? I didn't have those answers, but I had no other choice if I wanted to live, and I did. My past was drifting further away, making it harder to suck me back in. People were being placed into my life who would support sobriety.

The real challenge was re-learning how to integrate into society as a normal functioning, social human being, because I'd been drunk since the age of fourteen. The devil sat on one shoulder telling me lies about how I could control myself, while the angel on the other side told me I had the right idea about abstinence. One drink always led to more, not always that moment or that day, but I'd need to have more, more, more. I took advice from other alcoholics; I did what they did because they had control over their lives, or so it seemed. The key to their sobriety was realizing that they had no control. My past had proven that my poor choices couldn't keep me sober; I had to accept guidance from others. My attempts to cut back only led to more disastrous outcomes, so I had to choose ZERO alcohol, not a drop, not a sniff, nada. No vodka-filled chocolate, no cough syrups containing ethanol, and no toasting champagne to bring in the New Year. I would learn to read labels, menus and toast with water. I treated this like life and death because that's exactly what it was.

My mission became clear, and once my mind was set, no one could change it. Liquor was not essential to my diet, so I would not be harmed by eliminating it, and alcohol did not need to take up space in my cupboards or fridge, unlike food. *How would I cope with this new life?* Other people lived without it, and tomorrow I may worry about that, but not today. One day at a time and, sometimes a minute at a time.

Alcohol is my addiction, but when I ended the drinking, I avoided all drugs and medications that *could* become addictive. I did not want to risk any triggers for alcohol. I have an all-or-nothing perspective, which is a common trend amongst alcoholics; although, not always a helpful outlook. Sobriety and my body were my responsibility, and I started to care about my temple. The destructive booze brought nothing but chaos and pain into my life, so I let it go, one day at a time. I love the Alcoholics Anonymous mantra, "One day at a time." This helps to put things into perspective and reduces thoughts of helplessness to a manageable hope. I tried to focus on daily tasks that synergize with my sobriety, like exercise and writing.

Mentally, my resolve was firm, but this likely would've all crumbled if my environment was not set up for success. Early on, if I had visited the romping grounds or the bar scene, I would have failed. I needed an alcohol-free zone, and I had it. Most of my drinking buddies faded out of my life, and I focused on my supportive circle. Gary was dry, my friends never drank in front of me, and I had a few recovering drunks to lean on. I stayed close to my new clan to avoid the pitfalls.

One day led to another, and I was off to an impressive start, but without the ability to self-medicate my past tragedies, they resurfaced. The deep misery and shame I felt as a 12-year-old re-emerged from a hidden closet that I never expected. Gallons of coffee and sugary snacks were a substitute for losing alcohol, but they did not hide the pain that I believed to have under lock and key. The shame was rising, and I wasn't ready to deal with it. With months of sobriety under my belt, the brain fog was lifting. I saw the world in a different light; it was beautiful, real, and frightening, in a way I'd never experienced before. With the ascending skeletons, I wasn't sure I wanted to see it at all.

Chapter 24

# COMPASSION

Growing pains is never an easy process, but the result of being set free from past ghosts is worth the journey. The thought of having just one drink often crossed my mind, but I had to remember the sober days I'd been given were nothing short of a miracle. Someone up above thought I deserved a second chance. I never believed that life could be cool and fun without the drunk goggles on - food tasted better, the sun shone brighter, and the clouds seemed fluffier. This is the "high" of new sobriety; when you experience freedom from the heavy shackles that you've lugged around for too long. You are amazed and grateful to be free and now believe in happily ever after. Guess what? Despite my high hopes, that's not how it went.

Painful memories came back to haunt, and alcohol no longer numbed the pain. I'd spent the past several months sober, thinking past issues had died with my drinking, but they crept up, and I could not drink them away. True intimacy in my new relationship was challenging, as trusting a man and bonding seemed impossible. I had a lifetime of pain that kept me at a distance from people. My new sober friends advised me to deal with them. Facing fears and telling the truth would set me free. This is the message I'd been told many times. I would take one small step towards healing to remain sober.

Past demons constantly told me that I was no good, that I deserved all the suffering I'd endured. I was falling into my hole of relapse and had to take action. Facing them head-on was the only way to freedom. The guilt and shame I carried was a lie. A part of me could see that there was worth in me, somewhere. I reached out to God, giving him my addiction, and began a new relationship to help me on my passage; a personal one, a loving one of forgiveness and faith. He was my higher power, the one who would take the wheel and lighten my load. I could see no other way. My mom faced her pains and sorrows with faith, and I'd never seen anyone happier or more grateful than her. When I did the same, a journey of healing through counselors came to me.

A friend gave me a phone number and encouraged me to make an appointment, all by myself. In my weakness, I wanted her to do it, but she refused. If I truly wanted sobriety and healing, I'd have to take on responsibility and set up my life myself. Others can offer support and guidance, but the steps were mine to take. The phone number was on a small piece of scrap paper that I tucked away in my wallet for weeks. It took time for me to build up courage and ask for help from complete strangers, but finally, I made the awkward call. We discussed the process of counseling, and an appointment was booked. I was nervous. I didn't know how to interact as an adult. I hardly knew how to be a teenager as those years were taken from me. My drinking stunted my emotional development, and I had to learn how to function as a grownup. I was a 22-year-old adult with the mind of an immature 14-year-old. I had healing and catching up to do. This was my chance, an opportunity I wasn't going to miss.

I stepped into the office for my first counseling session, with my heart pounding, hoping I didn't forget to put on deodorant. A trip down memory lane terrified me, but it was a part of the process, they told me. I'd have to put on my brave face again. *I'm ready for this,* I hoped. The counselors, an older married couple, also pastored a church. People were drawn to them for their caring nature and accepting attitudes. Mrs. Cromwell was a dainty-looking woman with bright silver feathered back hair. She was a wholesome type. She took pride in housework, in caring for her family, and being a pastor's wife. Her demeanor was soft, and I trusted her immediately. Mr. Cromwell was very much like her, happy and gentle-natured. He was much taller than her, a suit and tie kind of guy. His hair and small mustache were also silver. Mr. Cromwell was the head of the household, but his wife received a great amount of respect from her husband. They were a two-person team, each equal and valued in their different roles.

They did not rush my healing. Mr. Cromwell guided the sessions and gave homework, while his wife gave moral support. Several months of sexual abuse counseling passed and burdens lifted. I started to place the guilt where it belonged, on Ronnie. I wished he had beat and gagged me, physically forced himself on me; that way, I'd have less self-blame. It would take years to repair a broken spirit and forgive myself, but I was on my way. My drinking also hid memories about my dad, only a few years passed since his death, and I hauled around enormous guilt. Our entire seventeen-year relationship was dysfunctional, and the chance for resolution never came.

Slowly, I became open. I started from the early unpredictable days of home life with my father to his last weeks on earth. With honesty, I talked about his anger and punishments and how they affected me. They listened to the rubber hose stories and leather belts—his coldness. Half of me felt guilty for talking negatively about the departed, while the other half lifted to freedom. Dad did not know how to be a father, and suffered himself with mental health issues, but he was the dad given to me - sobriety changed my heart. God gave me the courage to start counseling, to trust a male, a father figure. I was honest about family secrets, the kind that families never want to be exposed, the kind I thought should die with me, but for personal freedom, I would talk. *"The truth shall set you free."* John 8:32. I believed this whole heartedly, and I was desperate to be free, but how do I talk about so many sorrows? How do I discuss my dad's cruelties? It would take time. Mr. and Mrs. Cromwell gained my trust, I felt they would not judge a man they'd never met, and they had raised children of their own. Our sessions were for my healing, and I tried to be as honest as I could.

At one session, I told Mr. and Mrs. Cromwell a story about our bunnies. My dad built a basic cage from plywood and chicken fencing. It sat against a tool shed by the pond filled with straw and looked like a decent home. We got two bunnies, one brown and the other black, from neighbors down the road. The bunnies were still young, and Dad said it was my job to feed them. I was ten years old and able to feed them hay, pellets, and change their water dish. Johanna and I played with them often, and we loved petting their soft downy coats. We wanted to get them used to being handled. Johanna brought some of her doll clothes over, and we clothed them in dresses and necklaces. We gave them a little poof of powder for a finishing touch, and they were ready for the runway. We often had rabbit races in the sauna change room. We chose our racing bunny and placed them at the starting line, *3-2-1- GO!* The first one to cross the finish line, six feet away, would win. The whistle sounded; Johanna cheered Mr. Blackie to the red ribbon, tempting him with a carrot. Brown Bunny hopped along, aiming for the carrot I tried to lure him with, eventually, they would make it and get their reward. It didn't matter who won.

Brownie and Blackie eventually turned into a family of seven or eight. The mini ones were adorable, and I was so happy. *I wonder how they can all live in a small area?* I expected that another house would be built, but it didn't happen. Somehow, once the babies started hopping around their cage, most of them mysteriously disappeared. A dividing wall was added to separate the two rabbits. Dad bunny lived on one side and the mom and two babies on the other. There seemed to be enough room, and I took them out often for playtime. During the winters, insulation on the roof helped to keep them warm. Heavy blankets covered the front of the chicken wire. Most of the time, the bunnies hid in darkness, but on sunny days, the cover was opened so they'd get some sunlight. I wished they lived inside, in my bedroom, but Mom said they would stink up the house. They survived the winter, and the babies grew into adults.

One day I skipped my way down the driveway to play with my fluffy friends. The cage was empty and the latch open, but no bunnies were in sight. I searched around the pond, in sheds, and in the sauna. I was about to go tell Mom but decided to check the lean-to off the sauna; the entrance was only a partial wall. I walked in and found them. They hung from their feet, wrapped in bailing twine attached to ceiling hooks, all four-draining blood from their smashed in heads. I rushed to the house, crying my face off. Mom tried to assure me, "it's a normal part of life." I don't know what she meant, but our usual Mojakka (Finnish beef stew) did not seem the same. My dad made a wisecrack about the "bunny stew," so I dropped my spoon, left the table, and gagged in the washroom.

Mrs. Cromwell dried her tears, and I was glad I never told them about Puss. No one would be ready to hear that story. Mr. Cromwell took a deep breath before saying, "I'm sorry you had to witness that." As a child, I didn't know that people ate rabbits, I only knew that I had pets. Puss never turned into cat stew, so why would my rabbits?

Memories of my dream home in the country unfolded, along with the pain of leaving it behind. I really loved my house, but it was tarnished. We discussed how hard it would've been if I had stayed in the home where the abuse took place. The sauna would be a constant reminder of Ronnie on top of me, under the floral orange bed sheet. The dock by the muddy pond would have the image of Ronnie and I fishing and laughing while he was hatching a secret plan to take my innocence. Despite the loss of my physical freedom in the country, I'd already lost a freedom far more valuable that could never be replaced. Although escaping the place of reminders did NOT erase the traumatic memories, it somehow still protected me. I'm convinced I would've acted on my suicidal thoughts at twelve years old had I not been forced away from my home and into a completely different life. I didn't have all the answers, but I was finding that all things happen for a reason, and I had to put my trust in God, which would become a lifelong journey.

My heart started to heal through this painful process, which I never saw possible. The big burly gentleman and his petite wife came into my life to show ultimate compassion to a worthless lush. As I spilled my guts out about my experiences, and the shame it had caused me, he listened without interruption. She held my hand and they both sniffled, holding back tears as I spoke. Their compassion overwhelmed me, as I expected to get judgment from a man of God. Complete strangers genuinely sensed my pain and never doubted my words. The husband-and-wife team dried their eyes and apologized for their sniffling. *Apologize?* They'd just given me the greatest gift---deep empathy and acceptance. Even though I didn't see worth in me, they did, and that was all I needed for my heart to soften. I realized maybe I deserved more, and the world had a spot for me.

They provided many tools for my journey of healing. Counseling was important and very beneficial; I continued for months. I also read the big book from Alcoholics Anonymous and combined that with prayer, therapy and journaling. Some friendships ended, but the true-blue ones stuck; a new life was being paved, a clean slate. With a few years of sobriety now under my belt, I had made it past the age of 25, which I never imagined. I truly enjoyed what the world offered. My distorted brain faded away as I tried to tell myself the truth and re-phrase my self-talk. What consumed my mind became a reality. When I believed that I was worthless, I was. When I accepted my value, it was there. Action cannot happen without it consuming the mind first. I enjoyed life without alcohol, weekend campouts, fishing, 4x4 adventures in Gary's '68 souped-up truck, and playing pool were a few fun activities, but I still had a fierce internal struggle that disrupted life.

I failed miserably in math and quit college again. I found a job I thought I might like at a hotel, but on the first day, I had a panic attack and never returned. I tried and failed many times, so I stopped trying. Everyone else did it; they did math, had jobs, and were not drunk. Others did life; what the heck was wrong with me? Sometimes I'd want to scream and bang my head against the wall. I let my high expectations for myself pull me down. I slowly grew and matured, but I still compared myself to others, which was not healthy. It didn't help when people told me how well others were doing, insinuating that I should do awesome too. They didn't know my past. As hard as I tried to be like everyone else, this only dragged me down further. At that point, I was alive and sober; it was a significant victory that I often forgot to tell myself.

Slowly, I grew. I was compassionate and much stronger than I realized. I had talent and skills. While I could barely add two simple numbers together without using my fingers, I could sketch a picture-perfect portrait of a loved one, and emphasize with the little girl who slashes her wrists in desperation. My life had value. Life tried to take me down, but I made it. I settled into healing, assuming the worst was behind me. I was wrong.

Chapter 25

# CRASH LANDING

I'm doing it. I'm growing up. The new me is in touch with my emotions, the good, the bad, and the downright ugly ones. I experienced bouts of depression but never turned to drink. Day by day, I became stronger. I started working in a department store and making my way in the world. Financially I shared in household responsibilities, and most importantly, I was gaining self-confidence and learning new skills. Gary's work took him out of town often, so I had the responsibility of caring for the home, which kept me busy. Our lives were stable and fulfilled, but we still had a missing part, a baby. With my past fears and fertility issues, I didn't know if it would be possible, but just as Gary and I started family discussions, I became pregnant. I was overjoyed, floating on clouds with a permanent ear-to-ear smile on my face! I had won the jackpot, and I deserved it. This time motherhood is mine; I would be a good mother. My body was healthy, and the timing was perfect. Our first step was to officially get married. Although marriage was a part of the plan for a while, I was more focused on the baby.

Weddings are supposed to be in a church, with flowing dresses, flower girls and parties. If my phobias about crowds of people were not so severe, I would have preferred a church wedding, but when eyes were on me, my entire body would visibly shake from fear - yes, it was that bad! My growing baby was my top priority, and I did not want to put him/her through that anxiety, so Gary and I agreed on a small gathering at an indoor conservatory that always had blooming plants year-round. We stood near a waterfall, and my brother-in-law, who was a pastor, officiated. Food and cake were served at my in-laws' home, and all local family members shared our day. Life could not be more complete.

There were many sleepless nights due to pure bliss and plans of all the future baby adventures we'd have. The first step was the ultrasound, where I would see my little bundle on the screen. The day arrived, at last, I was a glowing mama, thrilled to see the gift of life inside me. God himself could not wipe the smile off my face.

Gary was out of town working and could not make it to the appointment. I told him that there would be plenty of ultrasound appointments for him to attend, and I would give him a complete report as soon as I could. I asked Pam to come with me to my appointment. She was pregnant, and we would share the pregnancy journey together. Our children would be cousins of the same age. I attended the ultrasound with a full bladder. This gives the best viewing of the baby. *My bladder is exploding; hurry up and show me my little kidney bean, please*! Pam stayed in the seating area while I entered the dim room. I laid on the examination table, and the technician swirled and twirled the wand around my tummy for several minutes, taking pictures and scanning my belly at different angles. The screen faced away from me, but I waited to hear the first echoes of a heartbeat or any flutters.

The sounds of *lub-dub, lub-dub* didn't grace my ears. He delivered the worst news that every new mother fears, and said "I'm sorry, but I can't find a heartbeat." My ears noted what he said, but my essence left me, and I could not respond. With an expressionless white face, I stared at him. English was the spoken language, but the words would not sink in. He began to apologize and noticed my shock, so he gently repeated himself.

I was too stunned to react; there must be a mistake. Eventually, the door opened, and Pam realized that things had gone terribly wrong the minute she saw me. I bowed my head as we walked down the stairs instead of using the elevator. I didn't want to hear the whispers of the crowds:

*"She's the one who lost her baby. She probably deserves it. She would make a terrible mother."* I was convinced complete strangers had these thoughts about me. I could not face society; they were right.

Pam led me to her car. We were in the clinic parking lot and sat for a few minutes trying to make sense out of what had just happened. Tears of sorrow fell from her face as she apologized for my loss. My eyes were paralyzed. *What would I tell my husband?* I had to be strong until I was in his arms. When the shock faded, reality sunk in. I felt like I was plummeting from the sky, freefalling without a safety net. From the heights beyond the joyous clouds, I had been pushed off, uncoached about what to expect next. I was falling, and within seconds, landed so hard that I died - my spirit disintegrated into dust. Not even an inkling of trouble crossed my mind; everything seemed right. I was sober, a non-smoker, the perfect age, and I had Gary. I received a pivotal blow like no other. A drink would not be enough, I should just kill myself. How is this possible? My baby moved to Heaven, and that's where I longed to be.

I couldn't see myself making it through this, but thankfully my support team helped. They gave me hope, and every day, a reason to live. They encouraged mourning, and I was loved while I grieved; knowing I had help, phone calls and visits eased the pain of this difficult stage. Pam brought me a heart-shaped box and craft supplies to make a memory box in honor of my baby. I was robbed of any precious moments from two babies, so this was important for healing. The memory box served a few purposes; it kept my hands and time occupied; it forced me to grieve instead of running from the pain, and it would show the world that my baby existed. Inside, I placed, ultrasound pictures, a sleeper I bought, cards I received, poems, and a daily journal. I wrote about how deeply my precious one was loved, letters I would've shared with him/her in the future.

Although I longed for Heaven, I thought that if I had been pregnant twice, I might be able to conceive again. As long as a sliver of light existed, I had hope. Soon the day came when baby number three grew in my womb. I guarded myself while being happy and excited once again. There was absolutely no way this would go wrong, three times a charm. At first, the pregnancy was normal, but after a couple weeks, I drove to the hospital because of spotting blood – I was sure it was a common occurrence. I was determined to stay positive and do anything necessary to keep my baby safe. The triage nurse took my information, and I sat in the waiting room. I thought I'd be a top priority, being pregnant and spotting, but every name the nurse called was not mine. I started to panic, and my outlook began to change. Thoughts of losing another baby took over my mind. An hour passed, and smoke began to come out of my ears! I was disgusted at how pregnant women are treated; a last priority on the list. I couldn't take it any longer and marched up to the desk.

"Excuse me, I am pregnant and have been sitting here for an hour to get checked out. I am bleeding and might lose my baby!" I tried to sound threatening while still being respectful.

"Have a seat. The doctor will see you soon." replied the nurse.

Her response did not help. Miscarriages did happen, but I thought they should've at least humored me by telling me to sit with my legs elevated on a chair, give me a cup of water, a friendly touch on the shoulder; that's all I really wanted. Finally, blood work and an ultrasound confirmed my fears. Heaven gained another angel. Part of me blamed the nurse for making me wait, but it wasn't her fault. God would hear my wrath. My anger overshadowed my broken pieces. I was enraged at the stupid nurse, the rotten health care system, and God.

At this point, depression was seeping in. Doctors tried to assure me that miscarriages are common and should not affect my ability to have a healthy pregnancy. They claimed that there are many options still to explore, but I didn't want options, I wanted my babies.

Suddenly, a vision was again given to me. I can't explain why God graced me with his presence, but it made me yearn for Him more. Not just in a spiritual sense, but in a physical way. I wanted to be in Heaven, to experience his wonder and be with my babies and loved ones. I wanted the peace and bliss of our heavenly Father.

The vision: I'm laying on a hospital bed, eyes closed, unresponsive, surrounded by Gary, family and friends. Soft chatting echoes around the room while Gary holds my hand. A doctor enters and says, "it is now time." He is ready to turn off life support. *What? Life support? What's going on, how long have I been here? I don't want to go*. I hear weeping and my husband's grip tightens. The darkness from my closed eyelids grows darker and my family's voices are trailing off like the dial of a radio, until I hear nothing. I don't want to leave them; they are hurting, and I panic but cannot move. Soon there is nothing but silence, and the darkness lifts and light slowly emerges, I am leaving my body now. All things over the course of my life, quickly flash by me and then don't exist. Memories vanish; they've never occurred. From this moment forward, everything is new. I am leaving the old world for a new one.

Time moves faster; the light is getting brighter and my body trembles. I know this feeling. Am I in a tunnel or lost in space? I don't know. I can't see anything. My eyes are closed. Now the pressure is becoming intense, there's an urgency to go quicker, and the familiar trembling is surging through my body, if I had one. I am in the light of Jesus again, practically in His presence. At any second, we'd be face to face. I have no control over the excitement and the anticipation of being home with Jesus. I'm almost home free. The moment is finally here, I'm at Heaven's door, and Jesus is there; I know it. When I open my eyes, I will see what the entrance looks like. Will there be pearly gates? Maybe massive white beams with a golden padlock?

I open my eyes to see, and jolt upright to a sitting position on my bed. The glowing numbers on the clock read 3:08 a.m. The night is bright. Light from the moon and the stars shine on my headboard. My bed, my room: both are a huge disappointment. I am devastated to be there. My babes, Dad, and Marja were waiting for me. My soul was shown a place a million times better than any love or riches here on earth; it was at my fingertips.

I discussed this with the only person who would understand this experience, my mom. Jesus came to my house as a child, and now I went to His. My mom was excited about my journey and said that I'd been blessed again with His presence. I told her how powerful and beautiful Heaven will be, because the journey to get there fills us up with a joy like we've never experienced. She loved hearing about Heaven and Jesus. I didn't want to focus on my feelings of disappointment about being stuck here. I left it at that.

Depression settled in again. I was a self-loathing mess, a failure who still didn't belong. I only wanted to be in Heaven. I was debilitated and with the lack of energy, I was unable to work for fifteen months. The vicious cycle of not measuring up wouldn't rest; it circled my head continually. I carried the world by myself, and it was exhausting. I hid as much as I could, hoping others would not see how broken I really was. Seeking professional help was difficult because of shame, and I could not accept "crazy pills." Old fears of being outed as abnormal or psychotic lingered; I'd suffer alone. Forced smiles would appear to avoid any inquiring minds, but did they honestly want to hear my thoughts? I didn't think so. Depression was a miserable isolating existence, as I was young, talented and capable of anything, but misery was killing me. I tried to hide from Gary, but he knew the truth. There was nothing he could do; he hoped for it to pass soon. Without the alcohol in my life, when depression struck, it was severe, but I still chose not to drink. Physically my need for alcohol disappeared, but my thinking was like a pin-ball machine; all over the place. I could no longer drink my depression away, and I didn't like it one bit.

Somehow, after several months had passed, a dull ember began to glow at the end of the depression tunnel. I started counseling again at a local hospital where they offered different types of therapy. Not only did I have access to therapy, but I also had a great internist helping me with my diabetes. The shock from my pregnancy losses, and trying to maintain sobriety took its toll, so I needed help. I filled out questionnaires, talked about my past traumas and how I'd been able to stay sober for five years. I was diagnosed with clinical depression, had signs of bipolar 1, PTSD, and suicidal plans were in the works. I was asked specific questions about my suicide plot but held back some information. My therapist was a caring lady, but if I felt a need to escape the world still, I didn't want her to stop me. I reluctantly started antidepressants and antipsychotic medications, even though I believed this would confirm that I was a looney tune, but my life was on the line.

My long-term goal was to remain on my path of sobriety and start a family, so that meant therapy was my full-time job. Therapy was three times a week, and it took a long time to see that I was needed on this earth. A new pathway was carved into my brain. The medication lifted me up enough to make it through counseling, and I made it through a terrible low once again. I fell back into my role of caring for our home. I had joy, and I was ready for a fourth time to bring a baby into our home. It was not easy, but after testing and medications, we were blessed with a bouncing baby boy. Life was complete.

Chapter 26

# CHICKEN LEGS

Motherhood was a roller coaster I never expected. I didn't know it was possible to love another human so deeply. The look of his adorable smile when he saw me, made me fall in love. However, being a mother does not cure depression, and a child should never bear that responsibility. It would be an unfair burden to place on a child. My heart overflowed with love for my son, but depression still struck me down. At one moment, I was loving every day alive, the next moment, I was drowning in my familiar misery. Thanks to my rock, Pam, and others, I didn't stay down for too long. The chapters of my book of life started filling up with good times again. Sober ones.

My little family lived on the outskirts of town, in an unorganized township where we had privacy between neighbors, lots of greenery, and trees. During the winters, there were many places to snowmobile and snowshoe. My husband and I were both raised in the country, so it was natural for us to be living in a place like this. Our relationship still had struggles. Marriage was hard work; love was not enough. I had trust issues and still wrestled with low self-esteem, but we were on the same parenting page; our son came first. Our lives were busy, but we were grateful for our blessings and all the memories we were building. The peace and quiet of home gave me a sense of freedom, and boredom was a rare occurrence. There was never a shortage of things to do.

We had a log stove in the living room, so there were always chores for cutting, splitting, and piling wood. Sometimes the ancient copper pipes would freeze during winters and Gary would have to go into the crawl space to thaw them. Scattered traps in the cupboards were set for field mice, that tried to find a home, when the cold weather hit. The home was cute, even with the endless repair jobs. This place reminded me of the old farmhouse I lived in, but it was much cozier, and we had a complete indoor bathroom. Pam lived nearby and would often visit with her kids. The cousins entertained each other, while we had long gab sessions over a few pots of coffee about our thoughts and philosophies on life. No topic was off-limits. I shared all my secrets; *well, she'll know a few more after reading this book.* We were sisters-in-law, but sisters at heart.

Sometimes I had other visitors such as bears, skunks or porcupines. So, we had a BB gun to give the illusion that we would open fire if they didn't leave. The sound of a pop would scare them off into the bush. We also practised target shooting. There was something satisfying about hitting the bull's eye right on the nose. One afternoon I decided to step up my game and go hunting. I'd never done this before. Killing an animal was not in my blood, but I did kill fish and eat them, so I thought I could shoot a partridge - the wild chickens of the woods. I wasn't sure how to prepare fresh game, but I'd figure out that part later. Partridges were foolishly brave and slow. We could often see them meandering in the middle of the road as vehicles roared towards them; it's like they wanted to be killed.

I put on my boots, pink baseball cap and headed out with my gun. The BB gun was loaded with steel pellets, and I planned to wander around the house. The leaves were becoming scarce, and hunting season was approaching. Soon we would hear the echoes of a shotgun being fired in the area. The woods behind my home were dense with brush and had some swampy areas. Chipmunks scurried up tree trunks, chirping to warn their friends. *"Hide Alvin, here comes the blonde girl, and she has a gun!"* I could never shoot these adorable rodents.

## Box of Shame

The thick forest was getting too tough to walk through. The further I walked, the denser the bushes got. Any animal within miles probably heard me coming. I escaped the backyard jungle and appeared by the lawn, and just down the driveway, I saw the bird. There was my target on the other end of my car, I crouched and walked slowly towards the fowl, who waddled into the front bushes. These feathered creatures did not scare easily, every step I took, he took one until I reached the edge of the driveway. I propped the gun by my shoulder and aimed. POP! The pellet hit him straight in the head from thirty feet away. I raced to his side to see if he was okay, he wasn't. I shot once more to ensure he wasn't suffering. My first kill. My heart was pounding! I shuffled from foot to foot, unsure of what to do next. I didn't actually think my aim was so precise. I ran to the house and called my boss; he was the only hunter I knew who might be able to help. He especially liked to hunt for ducks. He told me what supplies to gather and to come to the store.

I quickly changed my clothes, grabbed a garbage bag, a knife, and a cutting board, then drove to work with the partridge. The mall was crowded with shoppers as I tried to zip past them to the eye glass store where I worked. A young male browsed the sunglass rack, I ignored him and turned the corner where only employees entered. My boss passed by me with a pair of glasses in his hands, “I’ll be right back, I can’t wait to see the bird.” I put the sack on the floor. I was getting excited about having my first lesson in de-feathering a partridge. We would slab up the pheasant in the stock room. My husband would be in for a surprise. The boss came to the back room. “I chained up the entrance and put up the back in fifteen-minute sign.” he said. I opened up the bag, and he looked in.

“Here ya go, what do you think?”

“I’d say this will make a nice dinner for you guys tonight. Good job.” I smiled and relaxed. A vision center wasn’t a place for butchering, but he wanted to help, and he couldn’t say no to the excitement of a fresh kill. I’d take the evidence with me, every little feather. He placed a garbage can near him and put the knife and board on the counter.

“How long does it take to pluck the feathers? I asked.

“We’re not going to pluck them.” He shook his head with a grin. He laid the garbage bag on the floor and spread out the wings of the bird. I stepped closer, expecting that I would prepare the chicken myself, after all, I’m the one who shot it. “Do you want to do this? It’s fast and easy, you just step on the wings and pull up by the legs." I took a step back.

My eyes widened. "Are you serious?"

"Ya, it's a quick move and you're left with a clean bird." he said.

"It doesn't sound clean to me. I don't think I can do that." The thought freaked me out a little.

"Alrighty, I'll do it." He got into position. He stood on the wings with his dress shoes and had a firm grip on the legs while he pulled up slowly, bones and tendons cracked, sending heebie-jeebies up my spine.

My shoulders tried to cover my ears and I crinkled my nose. There was nothing left but a bundle of feathers, chicken legs and a head dangling by its throat. As a meat-eater, I knew butchering was a part of the process, but I would never work in a meat factory. He began to de-bone the bird, carving out breasts and saving the little legs. I backed away to the entrance, peaking into the store. No one was waiting to come in, thank goodness. The room filled with an awful stagnant stench of rotting flesh. I pinched my nose with my shirt as my eyes watered. *Does he not notice this?*

"That is the most disgusting thing I've ever smelled!" I said. I worried that the stench would seep out into the store area, scaring off customers. They'd wonder what kind of sick place this is, and run for their lives. Well, it was his store, not mine, so I didn't worry about it when he didn't. He bagged up my meat and scraps.

"Come on, it's not that bad, you get used to it." He teased.

"Thanks for double bagging it. I hope it doesn't taste as bad as it smells." He gave me a few cooking tips before I left and assured me this would be the best meal I'd ever had. I cooked it like barbecue chicken. Gary was impressed, and we enjoyed a delicious dinner. The next day, I packed him left-over partridge breast and legs. At work, he opened his lunch box in the lunchroom: carrots, granola bars, partridge breast and two boney legs. With a fork, he scraped off a few slivers of meat from the bones.

"What's for lunch Gary?" A co-worker asked.

Gary replied, "Oh, the usual, except for these dried-up chicken legs."

"You call those chicken legs? They look more like frog's legs. There's not much to 'em, eh?"

"No, the old lady shot a partridge at home. She didn't know what to do with it, so she took it to her boss, and now I have overcooked boney little legs for lunch."

His co-worker laughed and said, "Well, at least you got a home-cooked meal. I have P&J, and I had to make it myself." I wondered if Gary realized that I would kill for him, literally. No sloppy peanut butter and jelly sandwiches for my man!

Chapter 27

## SURPRISE VISIT

I worked at the eyeglass store for six years and enjoyed it, but it was time to move on. A friend told me about an opportunity to attend school for a Personal Support Worker program offered by the government. There was a high demand for PSWs, and this initiative would encourage people to apply. Tuition would be paid for, as well as childcare expenses, and the cost of living. In addition, this education would give me the required certification to work with the elderly in different capacities. Much of my family worked in health care, so this was a chance to join the trend.

I took the first step and inquired about the details. Doubts lingered in my mind, and becoming a student was terrifying. As much as I enjoyed reading and learning, it was a struggle to stay focused because of my anxiety. I had a tremendous fear of failure, which caused me to give up school in the past. Self-doubt has a sneaky way of destroying growth. Taking chances into unknown territory is something I was not comfortable with by any means. My childhood chaos created a need for consistency in adulthood; I craved stability. I needed details to prepare for any unwanted surprises.

Free education was a once-in-a-lifetime chance, and I knew I had to take it. BUT there was always a but, a what if. Negative thoughts and fears could overtake me, and I could blow this whole opportunity. I had to believe this was the path for me and tried to think positively. This accomplishment would validate that I could become a positive part of society, making a difference to others. My past left me with some damage and scars, but I'd made it this far so I wouldn't waste this free gift. There were also peeping little eyes on me, learning from my example, and that finalized my decision to sign up. I fully expected this to be a challenge; life had thrown enough punches to make me realize that the unexpected can happen at any time, but I would be prepared to deal with it, with life's blueprint in hand. I tried to stay one step ahead to feel secure and safe in life.

After much contemplation and planning, I started the compressed six-month program in March, the year of a freak ice storm that shut down the entire city. It was a school day, and the roads were covered in grooves of ice, along with everything else in existence. The streets looked like the rolling waves of the ocean that suddenly froze. I skated to my truck from the front door and drove just past my mailbox up a slight hill. The tires of the truck caught the groove and the truck slowly crept backwards; braking was useless. It stopped when it hit level ice. I should have stayed in my cozy home, but if there was a way to get to school, I had to find it. Gary was at home, and he was able to maneuver the truck through the treacherous roads all the way to the school campus. My tenacity prevailed, and I made it to school that day. Mother Nature would not prevent me from a Perfect Attendance Award. A few other stubborn pupils stood by the locked doors when I arrived. They had the same streak of determination I did. The ice storm knocked out power, the streets became skating rinks, and class was not in session.

The classroom part lasted for three months and was followed by field placement for the remainder of the program. I felt comfortable in the class with a split of young and mature students. I did my work diligently and graduated on the honor roll. A sober victory and a proud day.

I started working in a long-term care facility, assisting the elderly with their daily personal needs. Health care was always a distant thought but drinking stood in the way of taking that path. Now with sobriety, dreams became reality. Finally, I was helping those in need. The work was stressful, both physically and mentally. The staff-to-resident ratio was unrealistic, especially when short-staffed, which was a common occurrence. Stress levels were high, but the work crew always pulled through, and we did our best for our elderly residents. I loved them and respected them for the simple fact that they were my elders and deserved it. I worked this job for two years and then spread my wings into community care, assisting the elderly in their homes.

I joined the team at Caring Hands. They offer personal support to folks to allow them to stay in their homes, as long as possible. The pace and environment differed from what I'd become accustomed to in long term care. I switched from an institutional setting, to stepping into peoples living rooms all day long. The work schedule had flexibility, which was nice because I had a toddler at home, and it was a lighter workload. Staff-to-client relationships became much more personal because I had more time allotted. Since I never met my grandparents, I missed out on that special bond that my friends had with theirs. My clients treated me like family, and although I had to respect professional boundaries, I loved them like grandma and grandpa.

I enjoyed my work. My calm disposition and gentle approach made clients feel at ease. Once relationships formed, both clients and I felt more comfortable. I like consistency and routine; it's my safe bubble. One morning, while I looked at my assignments for the day, a familiar name and address appeared that I hadn't thought about in years. The past stayed far behind until it came to shake me up, a blast I didn't expect. The name was Mrs. Brunetti, on Melbourne Drive, and immediately, I froze. Surprise, guilt, grief, curiosity; it all swept through me at once.

I rearranged my schedule to visit her last, or I may ask to have another worker see her. I asked my manager to give me all the information she could about Mrs. Brunetti. I found out she had only been with our company for five months and still functioning well in her home as a widow. Her mind was intact, but would she remember me after so many years had passed? Did I want her to recognize me? I was confused and needed the morning to mull it over. Yes and no, bounced around my head. Finally, I decided I would visit Mrs. Brunetti, because if I refused this assignment, I'd have to explain my reasons to the manager - I did not want to broadcast that part of my past. I'd been in plenty of uncomfortable situations in my field of work, which I handled well, so I could do this. Off to Melbourne Drive I went.

I arrived at the off-white brick home and parked on the street beside the house. The apple trees were still there, but the fence was now chain-link fencing, and there weren't many plants growing. The shed behind the house still stood, and a car missing a tire sat in the driveway, even though she never drove. I arched the rear-view mirror down for a quick makeup check and took a deep breath in and out before exiting. I tapped lightly on the storm door. If she didn't answer, I would write, "Client not home" on my report, and I'd avoid the entire situation. The interior door was wide open, and I saw a chubby little Italian lady approaching me, smiling and waving me in before she reached the door. "Hello, hello, nice to see you, come in," she said as she pointed to the chair at the kitchen table. *Did she recognize me? She'd only seen me for ten seconds.*

I smiled at her and sat down on the chair she pointed at. "It's nice to see you too. My name is Anita from Caring Hands." I studied her facial expression to determine if there was a spark of any kind when I stated my name. Nothing. *Thank goodness.* With her broken English, she started talking about a worker she had the day before who helped with laundry and gave her medications. Most of the housework had been done, and she only wanted me to vacuum. I lost interest in her idle chatting as I felt the need to explain myself. I did not know how she would react or if she would remember me, but I cared less and less about her reaction, I was in her home and I couldn't pretend we were strangers. Secrecy had proven to only cause harm throughout my life and whether she spat on me or hugged me, I would leave knowing I cleared the air in truth.

She finished her story and then said, "Can you vacuum there?" She pointed to the living room behind me. I glanced over my shoulder towards the unused sitting room that still had the plastic covers on the sofas, that they never allowed kids to sit on.

"Yes, of course I can." I replied. I cleared my throat and let the words, "Do you remember who I am?" fall out of my mouth.

"I tink I see you here before, last week?" *Maybe in the 1980s.*

"No, Mrs. Brunetti, it's Anita, I used to date your son, Tony, in high school."

Her eyes lit up in excitement, "Yes, I know tat!" she leaned in for a hug and I stood up to get closer for the embrace. "It's long time for me to see you." I knew she accepted me, and the drunken episodes under her roof were all forgotten. I vacuumed her immaculate living room carpet while I looked at her cherished photos of her children on the walls.

Mrs. Brunetti caught me staring at the portraits. "Tony's such a good boy. He come to visit me all da time."

I couldn't help but give her a warm smile, knowing that her son took care of her. My last task was a medication check. I popped out her evening pills from the blister pack and put them in a dish. "Don't forget to take these at bedtime," I instructed.

"Yes, yes," she replied. My time was now up, and I'd be on my way. Mrs. Brunetti was preparing coffee and set cookies on the table. "Sit." she said. When an elderly Italian woman offers treats and tells you to sit, you do it.

She was my last client of the day; a few extra minutes would be fine. She spoke lovingly about Tony and her family. The kitchen table was not the same one I remembered; this table was a round light maple color. The old one was a rectangle shape with a tablecloth that used to be filled with food and wine. This is where I sat and was taught how to eat spaghetti the "right" way by

Mr. Brunetti - with a spoon and fork. This was where I listened to an Italian family hollering at each other in love, as I raised my wineglass to cheer them because I didn't understand the language. I chased away my demons that nobody knew about with the bitter red wine at this table. A slight shiver trickled up and down my spine, remembering the broken little girl in this house.

She pushed the plate of biscotti cookies towards me and poured coffee into a fine China teacup. I filled my cup up with a lot of sugar and cream because I'd given up coffee but didn't want to seem ungrateful. She wanted to show her appreciation for my help and enjoyed our chit-chatting. She welcomed me back anytime, but I sensed I would not visit again. I stood at the exit looking down the long staircase, and the image of my dad carrying his suffering child up these stairs flashed before me. Peace and sadness filled my heart. Before I walked out the door, I gave her a message, "Tell Tony, Anita was here and said hello." I hugged her, and she handed me a bag of baked goodies for the road. "Si, I tell him. Tank you." She tapped me on the head as I turned away.

Chapter 28

# CLOSURE

I stood outside on the concrete slab, looking towards my car, before stepping down the two stairs and onto the grass. My vehicle was in the same spot my dad parked when I nearly died from alcohol poisoning. He came here to save me from myself. Visiting the place where my drinking roots began and facing my ex-boyfriend's mother was awkward but envisioning my sixty-four-year-old dad carrying me, because I was too drunk to walk, pierced my heart. Imagining my own child here, hurting so deeply that only a state of oblivion could ease their pain, forced me to see what my dad experienced. I hung my head walking without him. I left with sadness for the little girl who had to drown in wine for so long. I went through the motions; I turned on the car, put it in drive, checked for traffic and went. Without fully realizing my direction, I must have had a need for home, and I began driving to my parent's house, even though Dad would not be there. Mom would be there to greet me with her warm smile, and comfort is what I needed.

Much of the route I drove was the same as it had been years ago. The mini mall where I vomited in the truck had expanded, the houses were the same, but the trees on the lawns had grown, hiding the sunlight. As I drove, I got lost in thoughts of Dad, no longer hearing the radio. I thought I had grieved all I could for him, but my eyes found more tears. Escaping my drinking years was an accomplishment I never thought possible, and I wished for my dad to be a part of it. My father could be ruthless, disregard the needs of his children, yet I longed for him at this moment. With sobriety and healing, I finally realized that my dad was exactly the dad I wanted, if only for a moment. Days before he left this world, he showed love and regret over his past behaviors. With years of healing, my heart had room for forgiveness – perspective is everything.

Peace filled my heart, but I couldn't help but carry the loss of him; he would never be able to witness how my world turned out. He would never know why I struggled, my family would never meet him, and he would not hear the word "Pappa" from my son. He would never see me reach sobriety or the insane amount of stress I went through to become a registered practical nurse. Some tell me that my dad knows I found peace, but I'm not sure; he is far too busy and overjoyed in Heaven to be looking down on me.

I pulled into Mom's driveway, walked inside, and her face lit up from my presence. I never talked to her about Dad seeing me drunk for the first time; that was between him and me. Right now, I was forever grateful for this woman who never gave up throughout her days of grief and depression. She was now full of love, strength, and forgiveness. I kept my promise to Dad, to God, and myself. My last parent would never leave earth without knowing that I loved her, and she did not.

Mom joined Dad 25 years later. They have no pain; their souls are free, and I know I will see them again. I picture Dad operating the skidder of his dreams, logging trees in the golden forest. Mom is growing magnificent gardens of vegetables and flowers. God has blessed them with an eternity of work, and their hearts are full. Their two younger children skip down the streets of gold, safe and happy. The angels are pampering Marja. They brush her flowing waves of hair and magically add a splash of pink to her lips; she is whole. I know they are all living souls, and although I miss their physical touch, I am calmed by thinking of our sweet reunion to come when my journey is complete.

At 14 years old, Dad scolded me in the kitchen about alcohol being poison. I now must agree with the crazy old man. If I drink it, I will die. And that is how I've achieved my years of sobriety; a lesson Dad left with me.

# EPILOGUE

The dysfunctional relationship I had with my dad will be fully restored in Heaven. I no longer allow guilt about his death to eat me up. I live every day thankful for life. I finally learned that forgiving gives freedom and that I was worthy enough to be free.

Through reflection of a chaotic life, I recall seeing a full-grown man covering his ears, during our playtime, screaming, “STOP THE NOISE!” To me, he looked like a baby, but I realize now that PTSD (Post Traumatic Stress Disorder) is a serious mental health disorder and, without treatment, can be dangerous. I believe he suffered from this because of World War Two.

Pam and I remain close friends through our busy lives. We do not always share the same struggles, but our bond is strong, even while being distanced through our Covid 19 pandemic. She is still my rock, always has an open ear, and is the one person who is not afraid to voice her opinion or give advice in love. I respect and admire the woman she has become.

Johanna’s journey took her throughout many cities in Canada and the United States. She did not return to live in our city. I'm sure she would have an amazing story to tell if she chose to. She has visited Thunder Bay over the years, and although our lives went in opposite directions, I love our get-togethers.

Ten years or so after I left Randy, I found out he committed suicide. None of the old gang was surprised, but it was sad news; a life was lost. He remained tormented by his demons, never able to escape. During our drinking days, we often listened to Alice Coopers, "Skeletons in My Closet." Randy would never delve into what those skeletons were, but I think they were similar to mine, and we both used alcohol to keep them hidden.

In 2003, I gave birth to a healthy son, the light of my life. He was planned but came at an unexpected time. I once again did not know I was pregnant. I was given the shocking news while having an ultrasound for another purpose. I was being taught a lesson about control, again. *Anita, you have no control. Live in today and do not worry about what tomorrow may bring.* One day it will sink in, I hope! My boy's birth was long and stressful. After hours of hard labor, an emergency cesarian section was needed. There was no time for epidurals; I was knocked out like a light when the most breathtaking baby entered the world. He was alive and healthy; I am blessed far more than I deserve.

After a few weeks of recovering, I saw my doctor for a follow up and she had some interesting news for me. As the nurses cared for my baby, she held my uterus in her hands and noticed the shape of a heart, it seems two wombs were growing and combined into one, leaving a slight indent. She put my organ back in place and stapled me up. A slightly misshapen uterus made maintaining a pregnancy difficult, but love and prayers kept my son thriving for nine months. My bundle of joy was living in a house of love. My sobriety has continued without any relapses. A miracle! Sober, yes, but I have to admit that my lips once tasted alcohol, and it was a terrifying time!

I attended a service at a church that I was not familiar with, and it happened to be communion day. I'd taken communion many times in my home church. We eat the flesh of Christ and drink the blood of Jesus, metaphorically speaking. The flesh is usually crackers, and the blood is grape juice, but communion at this other church was done with wine. I knelt at the altar with my ten-year old son and received the gifts from the pastor. He prays, and I slam back what I assumed was juice. In shock, my hand slams my mouth while the other smacks my kid. "Don't drink that!" Poor boy didn't know what was going on.

The pastor sees a fuss happening and approaches us at the alter. “Is everything ok?” “I’m sorry, but I didn’t expect wine!” I stare up at him, eyes wide and embarrassed. This clearly was not a regular occurrence in this church.

“I apologize. There is grape juice available if you’d prefer.” I thank him for the offer before leaving the alter to sit at my pew. The entire purpose of communion was lost, as I could not believe that I’d drank wine after many years of sobriety. He closes the service, and the congregation begin lining up at the door, when we reach the exit, the pastor is there, and I apologize to him again and tell him the truth.

“My lips have not tasted a drop of alcohol years. I am a recovering alcoholic.” He looks stunned and concerned, so I quickly add, “But I’ll be fine, it just surprised me, that’s all. Don’t worry.”

From that day over the next few weeks, I was in panic mode, on high alert with every thought, craving and self-talk that was going on in my head. Sobriety comes first, and I HAD to monitor myself with a microscopic lens. Time passed, and I did not fall into relapse. This is what must be done to maintain sobriety—and asking if communion is done with alcohol or juice. Lesson learned.

## Box of Shame

I am a survivor of trauma, chaos, and addiction. I felt worthless, but kept moving forward, enduring blow after blow to tell this story. Secrets once stole my freedom, but now, my box of shame has busted open. I am no longer sick in my secrets. I am free.

I wish for you hope and healing.

# ACKNOWLEDGMENTS

Writing a book is no easy feat! I never imagined all the work, time, and tears that would go into this project. It began as an innocent need to journal some thoughts, but ignited into months of deeply personal writing. I felt compelled to dig deeper and type the words from a traumatic past that I never dreamed I'd share with the world. I know this story is not meant for the grave. I have set it free.

Special thanks to my long-time friends, Bobbi and Monica. Bob, without your support and prayers, I would not be here. You have literally saved my life more than you know! Your love and support are priceless. I am forever grateful for our friendship. Monz, I cherish our childhood memories. The horses, our adventures, and our "spaz attack" days; your friendship, truly lit up my darkest days. Love both of you gals!

To my fam - I appreciate your hand in raising me. Although life went spiralling down later, you have given me many memories to cherish. We all know that us Finlanders aren't openly emotional, but I can offer you these true words: I love you all! And that is as mushy as I get!

To Sarah Cannata, who was the first person outside of my circle, to read my first very rough draft, and I mean rough, thank-you. Your guidance encouraged me to tell my story in greater detail. Thanks for steering me into the right direction; I had no idea what I was getting myself into.

Thanks to all my wonderful beta readers, you know who you are. I'm sure there were at least a dozen of you. Your honest comments were so appreciated. You boldly told me when boredom overtook you and when emotions hit your heart. You have all helped to make this book what it is!

My deepest gratitude to Danielle Anderson, book coach and editor, you pushed me deeper into the important heart matters of this story, even when I didn't want to go there. Your expertise in seeing fine details to make the story flow, is amazing. There are no slipping things past you, you will find it, and question it. Thank-you for caring about my story and sharing your passion for memoir.

To Katie Everette for your editing expertise and kind words. Thank-you for the final touches and help with putting everything together. I was fortunate to have you join my writing journey. I appreciate you.

Thanks to Marlowe Boyd, for your editing and prompt services. I am glad to have found you.

Finally, thank-you God. Without your hand in my life, I would have been lost forever. My greatest blessing, my son, is here because of YOU. Well, maybe my husband also had a little something to do with that … husband; thanks for our life.

# ACTIVITY PAGE

I am a lover of memoir, and true-life stories of struggle to victory. If you have read this far, I assume we share the same love of reading. I have one last thought for you… has this story awoken something within? I welcome you to share your overall feeling on this page, as a simple hand drawn picture. Stick figure, emoji style, scribble or elaborate scene are all acceptable. You may take a photo of your "feelings picture", and email them to me at anitakball@yahoo.com. I look forward to seeing your lasting impressions! Please take note, I WILL NOT, release your work or name on social media, without your written permission. If you do consent, you may find your work on Facebook, Instagram or on anitaballauthor.ca.

# MY FEELINGS

# ABOUT THE AUTHOR

**anitaballauthor.ca**

Anita grew up with freedom to roam, dusty dirt roads, and horses. The country is where she fell in love with art and writing. But, despite the spacious and peaceful surroundings, life wasn't always bright and sunny for Anita. Decades later, she's emerged from the darkness to tell her story of a traumatic childhood and battle with alcoholism.

Anita hopes her story will help shatter the stigma of addiction. Today, she has twenty-five miraculous sober years. She is truly thankful to God for every sober breath. The peaceful surroundings of country life in Canada are still home to Anita, her husband, and her son. She enjoys nature, cuddles from her giant fluffy cat, and two adorable mutts.

www.ingramcontent.com/pod-product-compliance
Lightning Source LLC
LaVergne TN
LVHW051254080426
835509LV00020B/2963
*9781777637439*